DADDY'S GIRL

DADDY'S GIRL

MARILYN SANDBERG GRENAT

DADDY'S GIRL

iUniverse books may be ordered through booksellers or by contacting:

iUniverse
1663 Liberty Drive
Bloomington, IN 47403
www.iuniverse.com
844-349-9409

ISBN: 978-1-6632-6639-2 (sc)
ISBN: 978-1-6632-6641-5 (hc)
ISBN: 978-1-6632-6640-8 (e)

Print information available on the last page.

iUniverse rev. date: 01/20/2025

CONTENTS

Introduction vii
Foreword xi
Dedication xiii
Epigraph/Purpose xv
Daddy's Girl xvii

Chapter 1 America's Scandinavian Beginnings 1
Chapter 2 Marilyn's Rough Beginning 11
Chapter 3 Oddities Remembered and Necessities Forgotten 17
Chapter 4 WWII Time (1937-1945) 22
Chapter 5 Starting a Different Foreign Life (1946-1947) 25
Chapter 6 The 1950's 38
Chapter 7 Our Swedish Trips (1954, 1960, 1975,1992, 2013, & 2022) 54
Chapter 8 My First Husband-Leon(1962-1977) 67
Chapter 9 Flying Experiences (1975-1977) 84
Chapter 10 My Second Husband-Vernon (1979-1981).. Country Living 92
Chapter 11 My Working Years – 1975-2003 97
Chapter 12 Our Swedish Traditions And Holidays 103
Chapter 13 Our Family Grew with Family and Animals 113
Chapter 14 Trips & Excursions With Family Skiing 130
Chapter 15 My Third Husband – Bernard "Gene" Grenat 1990-2010 140
Chapter 16 Grandchildren & Great Grandchildren 147
Chapter 17 Girl Friends & Boy Friends 1946-2022 152
Chapter 18 Love And Lessons Learned 160
Chapter 19 Family Fashion Sense 166

Chapter 20 My Dad's Work Influenced My Work 171
Chapter 21 My Business As A Caregiver For The Young &The Elderly 179
Chapter 22 Different Perspectives – Through Others' Eyes 184
Chapter 23 Finality 195

INTRODUCTION

My autobiography of a self-made man's self-made daughter.

I am proud to be the daughter of my Swedish-born immigrant father. I haven't become famous nor did my father become famous. But he was famous in my eyes, as he was brave and accomplished a lot in a New World of beginnings. He never felt fear of failure and he always Persevered and Persisted in his dreams. Life is a slow process and he pushed through all his trials and he taught me to do the same both by word and by example. I maybe wasn't ever successful in the eyes of many, but I felt I lived my life to the best of my ability with the influence of good Christian parents.

I accomplished a few things in life that mean a lot to me. The Lord gave me the courage and strength to rear four beautiful, strong children that I adore.

I have been fortunate enough to see grandchildren and great grandchildren.

The Lord saw to it that I was able to publish two books with promise of one more after this one. As long as my memory and eyesight hold out, I will try to finish these four. The Who's Who book wants to put a brief synopsis of me in their book, so that's exciting.

I have tried to live by Philippians 4:6 which is "Do not be anxious about anything, but in everything, by prayer and petition, with thanksgiving, present your requests to God." And to be content with every situation in your life Philippians 4:11b. "Be content what- ever the circumstances." 12b "being content in any and

And to be content

every situation." And John 14:1 "Do not let your hearts be troubled, but trust in God; and trust also in me (Jesus Christ)."

As I watched my Dad and Mom in their lives, I tried to imitate theirs by being a model parent in the humblest of ways. I didn't always know everything either, but Dad's actions made me want to try my best and try to accomplish as much as I could even if I had to teach myself along the way. That's why I feel I am truly a "Daddy's Girl". In another context of love, I was also a Daddy's Girl as I was his only girl at the time I knew it. True there was another daughter I did not know about until later, but she has been welcomed by both my brother and me. Since she didn't get to grow up with him or us, it was a mute point.

My actions and reactions definitely were similar to my Dad's in that I strived to accomplish all I could in this cometimes cruel, rough world. I felt I had to succeed after being forced into divorce and a life alone to rear four children. In a way, without their father in it, it was almost easier to rear them the way I saw fit without interference.

I brought them up in church and tried to keep family life as wholesome and normal as possible. The good Lord saw fit to help me provide a decent home near schools, and clothing and food no matter how humble.

I brought them up in church and tried to keep family life

I think it taught all of us to love and stay close and be thankful for all that He provided for us. He gave me strength for two jobs, and I think the kids were aware that He always provided for us and they learned not to take things for granted. It made them become good hard-working, accomplished, appreciative human beings. They were always loved, but never spoiled.

I'm very proud of my accomplished kids today. They felt education was important and always strived to be successful. While I have lost two husbands, I am still content to be in the arms of my Lord and Savior. My sweet Gene was a great world of joy, and taught me wonderful patience.

I am always a happy, contented person, love life, and love my family. I have been through a lot from losing the joy of my life, Gene, to Alzheimer's and my precious son, Jeff, to cancer. It encouraged me to write my first book, "Inspirations from the Heart" as a therapeutic poetry book and a blessing for me.

The second book was my Swedish immigrant father's biography - "Perseverance and Persistence". And from that comes my autobiography, "Daddy's Girl" of a man with perseverance and persistence that he taught me.

FOREWORD

To my mind it is unusual to be writing a Foreword to a book I haven't yet read. However, since my sister is the author it should be good because she's always been a storyteller; and I mean just that. When we were kids, her stories always seemed to get the attention she desired; especially with Dad since she was after all, Daddy's little girl. So let's see how it all plays out from her recollection or perspective now as a grandmother and great grand- mother of a four-year-old curious little boy, and a one-year-old boy and two more little girls who are now a year old as well. I'm quite sure that what is in store for us will be a kind of twinkling or winking of an eye in many cases; the kind that make you smile and say, "Oh sure! You'd better listen to this one; it ought to be a dussie!"

I hope it is a page turner for you. Enjoy your journey.

My sister's brother, Ralph Sandberg

Foreword-Ralph
Sandberg

DEDICATION

I dedicate this book to my children:

Annette and Dave Smith, Jeff and Joanna Fleeger, Kristina and John Oswalt, and Jennifer and Bob Delong.

And to my grandchildren Owen and Paige Patrick, River and Marlee, Kelsey, Brett, Harrison, and Charlotte Cohen, Emily and Jeff Zanker and Sylvia, Corrine Oswalt and Kandace Delong.

And to my brother Ralph and Kathryn Sandberg, and niece Jacquelyn Awes.

This is my autobiography and is one of my legacies I am leaving my family, so they will know some of their roots through my story.

With love from your mother, mormor (Momo), sister and aunt.

By Marilyn Sandberg Grenat

Romans 12:12 (NIV) "Be joyful in hope, patient in affliction, and faithful In prayer."

EPIGRAPH/PURPOSE

American author, Samuel Clemens (Mark Twain) once said, "Life is short, break the rules. Forgive quickly, rise slowly, love truly, laugh uncontrollably, and never regret anything that makes you smile." I suppose you might say I love life deeply and enjoy bringing a smile if I can to people – especially to my family. I love our ethnic Swedish background, and I am pleased to help my family learn from where their roots come. The purpose is to help them try to know and understand where and why their mom and grandmother is the way she is and to learn a little bit of the Swedish history, customs, and traditions.

When I was a little girl, I used to ask my mother to tell me about when she was a little girl or any stories she might know about her parents. I once got an "A" on an English composition I wrote about a story my mother told me about her mother (my grandmother). It was not only heroic I thought, but scary as well. Grandma Selma (Sally) took a shortcut to pick berries by taking a shortcut over the railroad bridge over the Wabash River, but when she got half way across, a train was coming and she knew she couldn't get to either end before it might reach her. So she let herself over the side holding on to the wooden slats and she felt the steam from the train on her hands. After it passed, she pulled herself up and continued on to the woods with her little basket and picked the raspberries in the woods. She then walked the long way home to be safe. A pretty brave little girl I'd say.

Hopefully you may have a smile or two, perhaps even a laugh at my life. Even though I've had some disappointments and even some tragedies in my life- time, I find remembering most of it I have not only enjoyed it but feel fulfilled in that God has always blessed me with tremendous rewards, and always provided for me and my four children. Dad's perseverance and persistence were instilled in me as well and we tough Swedes never give up. I pray that you may even have learned a few lessons to carry with you.

DADDY'S GIRL

Prenote:

It can be imagined by most that their lives are basically unimportant or un-Exciting to others. However, if you are forced to think back over your life you can Be induced to conjure up old feelings and responses that trigger emotions and remembrances that have brought you many pleasures. That special doll you wanted and mother said she couldn't afford or that bright, shiny bike under the Christmas tree that you thought you'd never get. I finally got one, but it was used. I didn't care. It didn't have to be new and shiny. When I was grown and out of college, my mother asked me if I still wanted that bride doll. I said no, but bought myself one a little later to use as a center piece for a friend's bridal shower. I rationalized it's purchase as something for a friend, but I still received the satisfaction of having one.

You perhaps remember that one friend who made you feel welcome in a new school, that guy or gal who smiled at you and made you feel special. That first kiss as a teenager that made your heart leap and your temperature rise because you don't really know if it was over embarrassment or the fact that you liked their attention. Feelings of affection can go on through the years until they lead you to the love of your life.

You develop friends through life that take you past graduation and reunions of old classmates and you build a considerable quantity of acquaintances through all your associations. Just reminiscing, you realize you can bring many wonderful memories to recall. In reviving your recollection you find you have some very stimulating remembrances to bring to mind. Your life was not as dull as you thought it might be.

CHAPTER ONE

America's Scandinavian Beginnings

Proverbs 13:22 "Good people leave an inheritance to their grandchildren" (NLT)

(and children).

And in my legacy, I am leaving a few "things", a few "dollars", and some stories of our family. When I was very young, I always wanted my mother to tell me stories of days gone by, especially of her and her earlier family. I don't know any kid who doesn't enjoy those.

I specifically enjoyed the one about her mother when she was a young girl and she was going on one of her excursions to pick berries. Selma (Sally) had gone many times before into the forest to pick berries, but the best spot was quite a distance. This particular day she was in a bit of a hurry and decided to take a short cut. This was a little dangerous, as it was down the railroad track bridge. This would cut off about an extra mile. With her little berry-picking basket she started her trek up and over the Wabash River onto the railroad bridge. She really didn't worry about a train coming, as she rarely saw one there. When she got half way over, she heard the dreaded sound of the train horn coming. She was half way, and knew she probably couldn't make it forward or backward before the train would be upon her, so she bravely let herself over the edge and held on to the wooden slats that held the tracks. She felt the steam on her hands as the train passed, but she nervously held tight until it passed and she then proceeded to pull herself up again onto the tracks. I can imagine how hard her little heart must have been beating. What an experience! She continued on across and picked her basketful of berries before heading home. This time she took the long way home to be safe. It was a while before she was able to tell her mother of the incident, for fear of being scolded.

This story amazed and amused me so much that I wrote an English paper on it, and got an "A" grade, and my teacher had me read it to the other kids in my class. They, of course, enjoyed it very much just like I had.

While my parents never met in Sweden, they both had Swedish roots. My father, Leonard Sandberg was born in the province of Småland in Southern Sweden and his parents stayed there while he came to the United States in 1926 at the age of twenty-three to make a better life for himself. His Swedish-American cousin, Carl Carlson, sponsored him so he could come and he sent him a ticket which Leonard paid him for as soon as he started working.

Leonard was a toolmaker at first which he had learned in Sweden in his father's blacksmith shop in Haurida, Sweden. Dad worked at that in Lafayette, Indiana, Chicago, Illinois, Rockford, Illinois, and Detroit, Michigan.

He had a tenacious attitude of "can do" in his personality and never felt anything he intended or wanted to do was impossible. His tenacity was filled with persistence and perseverance. He was never without a job during the Great Depression, because he would try and do anything legal to survive. His perspective of what he could accomplish was born out of an idea beyond what others might have the idea to try or even dream up. He accomplished this later in two different jobs he created. He was quite the entrepreneur.

My mother's parents came from the same area in Sweden much earlier. Selma Sundling, my grandmother, came with her family at age three, and Algot Swanson, my grandfather, came to the United States in 1884 when he was seventeen. They met in the Swedish Mission Covenant Church in Lafayette and married in approximately 1895. They had five children: Stephen, Paul, Sylvia, Helen and Kenneth. There were eight children born of these five, and the cousins always had fun growing up together.

My father, Leonard Sandberg, and mother, Helen Swanson, met in the same church as Helen's parents and married there on June 29, 1935 in Lafayette, Indiana.

After my folks married, my dad received a wonderful job offer to work at Caterpillar Co. in Peoria, Illinois. Ralph, my brother, came along on January 15, 1937. My arrival was not so smooth.

As parents, we always hope to give good advice to our children, so in this next poem, I Tried to give the same good advice our parents tried to give my brother and me.

Here's one of my poems I wrote on January 10, 2018

"Listen Dear Child"

Listen to me dear child-
I gave you a great gift-LIFE,
But God gave you a greater gift-ETERNAL LIFE!

Don't waste this one without trying-
To grow and become something special without crying.

You can be proud to help others-
This would please all mothers.

You can be happy to cure incurable diseases,
Or perform in great releases.

You will be praised to choose a magnificent mate-
And then to rear your children not to hate.

Teach them good manners, courtesy, and respect,
And all mankind will give them no neglect.

God's love must be taught through scripture
In a Bible-based church with a mixture-
Of action and belief to give relief
To a family of many peoples who want no grief.

We must love all our neighbors
Just as ourselves not without labors.

Help the poor, the orphan, and help the widow.
This, dear ones, is a message to which I can say 'ditto'.

The Bible instructs to love and forgive our enemies-
As we struggle to make sense of these.

We need to honor and obey our Lord and parents,
Just because pleasing God is apparent.

Be patient and kind and peacemakers
To all mankind-even the takers.

Do not be proud, loud, or stay in a cloud.
Do not be rude, crude, or be a bad dude.

You will win favor with man,
If you keep your name the best in the land.

Be reliable, faithful, and true
In your friendships, work, relationships, and stick like glue.

Trust the Lord as your stronghold,
Even though we wear a blindfold.

Remember Christ Jesus died for us to have eternal life,
And this I know, because he did it with lots of strife.

Forgive others, even though they may not forgive you,
And do not always worry about giving them their due.

Take care of family members always,
Just to show them love on all highways.

Read your Bible every day and pray,
And let folks say-you're okay.

Listen to me dear little ones as I rave-
There's just one more thing I want you to know-

I love each of you just as though-
You were the only child I have.
Even the ones I lost
At a terrible cost.
All my babes in a row,
Are Annette, Jeffrey, Shawn, Mical, Lauren, Kristina and Jen-
And they I gladly would take in tow.
Now I've claimed them all by pen."

By, Marilyn Sandberg Grenat

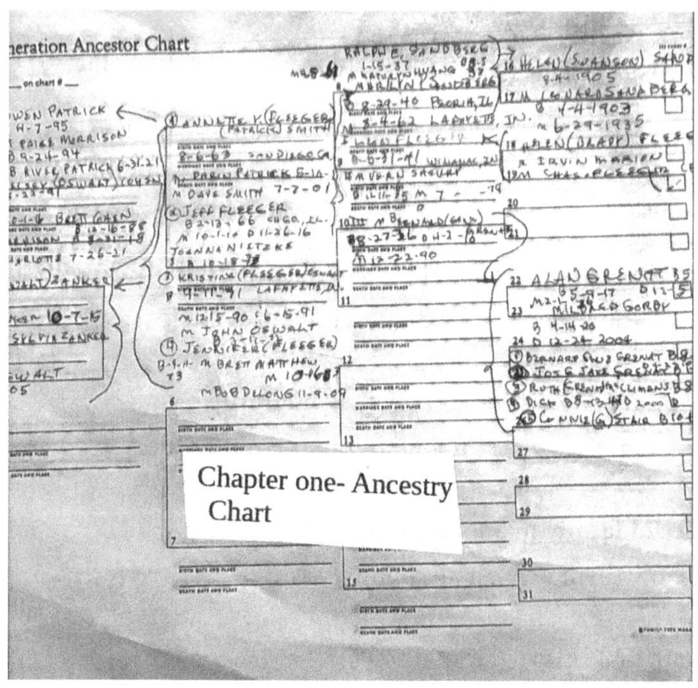

Chapter one- Ancestry Chart

Dad's homeplace in Haurida, Sweden

Dad's Parents ✓
(Klas & Kristina)
Sandberg

CHAPTER ONE

SANDBERGS ABOUT 1910

MAGNUS- LEN --GEORG- KRISTINA - HELFRI
(NILS) ELISABETH EINAR

Chapter one-Grandpa Sandberg the Blacksmith in Haurida, Sweden

Mom's Parents ✓
(Algot & Selma)
Swanson

Chapter One -My Mom & Dad
Helen &Leonard Sandberg

Chapter One – My
Brother Ralph & Kathy
Sandberg

CHAPTER TWO

Marilyn's Rough Beginning

Jeremiah 29:11(NLT)
"For I know the plans I have for you says the Lord. 'They are plans for good and not for disaster, to give you a future and a hope'."

Hebrews 11:40 (NIV)
"God had planned something better for us so that only together with us would they be made perfect."

Ephesians 3:20, 21 (paraphrased)
God has more for us than we could ever imagine for ourselves.

I believe God always knows what's best for us and He is in control-always.
I am content with whatever state I'm in and in all situations and circumstances.
I trust Him for His guidance. (Philippians 4:11-13).

Since my mother and I almost died at birth, I feel God must have spared Us because He had his own plan for both our lives. My mother was a loving, caring very capable mother, wife, helpmate and a fine Christian woman who went on to do many wonderful things for other people. She was a capable leader in many church organizations and she taught us to make wise choices and to choose our friends and companions carefully.
Prov. 13:20 He who walks with the wise and grows wise; associate with fools and get in trouble."
I Corinthians 15:33 (NIV)
"Do not be mislead: 'Bad company corrupts good character'."

Proverbs 18:24 (NLT)
"There are 'friends' who destroy each other, but a real friend sticks closer than a brother."

Psalm 39:4,5a
"Show me, o Lord, my life's end the number of my days; let me know how fleeting is my life. 5 You have made my days a mere handbreath."

My Poem "Life is Short" By Marilyn Sandberg Grenat Life is from the beginning definitely fleeting, Until we someday with Him will be meeting.
In God's eyes our life is but a twinkling of an eye And it will go so quickly before we disappear in the sky.
So don't waste it, but make something of yourself-
So that you and others realize you're not sitting on a shelf.
Be proud of your accomplishments and share them with others,
So all can be as happy achieving brothers.

I wrote this poem on 7-5-21

COMPANIONS By Marilyn Sandberg Grenat

"Choose your companions carefully,
As comradeship and friendship should not be dareful.

We must choose in the way of the wise,
Because we need good advice.

To choose good people to follow
Who's characterizations are not down in the hollow.
We need upright folks with integrity and conviction,
That we can copy with prediction."

Our folks decided to take Ralph on a little camping trip with the family before the new baby was to come the next month in September. However, Helen caught a cold which complicated her pregnancy, and the doctor gave her medicine which made her sick and did not agree with her.

She ended up having convulsions which resulted in eclampsia. This condition is not only serious today, but was extremely dangerous back in 1940.

She decided to stay in bed to rest after the weekend, and Leonard told her he would go downstairs and start the coffee and make he and Ralph a little breakfast. A bit later as he was going about these duties, he heard Helen screaming his name. He took two stairs at a time, but when he came upstairs, he could not find Helen. He finally located her on the floor between the wall and the bed. After he obtained her on the bed, she had another convulsion, so he rushed downstairs to call the doctor and the ambulance. After securing security for Ralph with neighbor Dorothy, he proceeded to receive the acceptance of the ambulance, which he followed to Methodist Hospital. Once he got there, the doctor told him he probably could not save both the mother and the baby. He asked him, "Which do you want me to save, the mother or the baby?" Leonard exclaimed, "Both, of course!" This was standard procedure to ask and Leonard wouldn't hear of anything short of a positive answer.

The doctor did everything in his power to establish success, and he was successful in accomplishing the feat. This was to the family's desire to attain.

This was a difficult task, as this little girl was a whole month early and only weighed four pounds and five ounces. It was touch and go for awhile, as there were additional complications.

They had to deliver her with forceps, and that damaged her earlobe with a bruise. Since she was underweight, they had to put her in an incubator, which, in those days, was heated with a lightbulb.

When they placed her therein, they positioned her ear close to the light bulb & The earlobe turn to a scab and eventually caused it to dry up and fall off. Back in those days, folks were not so sue-happy, and they were just happy to have Both mother and child live due to the circumstances. Since Leonard was a Mason, he decided to take his little girl to Shriner's Children's Hospital in Chicago, Il. to do plastic surgery on her ear to make it right again. However, they knew very little back then about that procedure to fix it right. It was a rather botched up job, but they would never right it, since Leonard had decided to take his family on a family trip to Sweden in 1946. They felt if he could afford to do that, then he could afford to pay for his daughter's surgery. So nothing was done because he probably felt if they couldn't do it right before, they maybe couldn't do it better now. She lived all her life with the ugly scars of them taking skin from her neck to make a mock earlobe that was never attractive or capable of having a pierced ear for an earring.

She grew up with never being able to have childhood pigtails, or teenage ponytails in her hair. So, I guess, she was just lucky being a girl so she could have long hair to cover her scars. It's OK after all, as that is all she has ever known. She would like to wear earrings though, as she is very feminine, and would like to be able to wear them.

On May 29, 1942 she was admitted to Shriner's Hospital and had two surgeries on her ear on June 11 and July 28, 1942. She came home 8-21-1942. She was admitted again 11-6-1942, had surgery & returned home on Jan.8, 1943.

Marilyn got Chicken Pox on July 6, 1943. She had it bad enough to itch a great deal and have a few scars.

On March 10, 1945, Dr. Owen took Marilyn's tonsils and adenoids out and she came home the next day with no problems. Children have childhood problems, however, we successfully outgrow them. I have been a very lucky girl to have only a few medical problems. I do feel the Lord has watched over me for many years and cared for my well-being.

I went to school to Kindergarten at White School in Peoria, Illinois, first grade in Haurida, Sweden in a one-room schoolhouse, second grade through twelfth grade in Lafayette, Indiana.

I got my Associates Degree from North Park College (now University) in Chicago, Illinois in 1960.

I got another Associates Degree from Indiana Paralegal Law Institute in Lafayette, Indiana in 1989 at age forty-nine.

I worked fourteen years at the Tippecanoe County Sheriff's Department handling

All the legal papers from the courts.

Then I worked sixteen years at Purdue University in Accounting. After I retired, I worked in homecare provision taking care of the young and elderly. It was a very satisfying job after I had taken care of my Alzheimer husband for eleven years and then started my own caregiving business. It gave my clients and me a great deal of satisfaction and ended up being my most rewarding job ever.

Family Picture 1945
Ralph 8 Marilyn 4 ½

CHAPTER THREE

Oddities Remembered and Necessities Forgotten

Proverbs 3:5 & 6 (NLT) 5 "Trust in the Lord with all your heart; do not depend on your own understanding. 6 Seek His will in all you do, and he will show you which path to take."
Psalm 100:4 (O.T. NIV)

"Enter His gates with thanksgiving and His courts with praise; give thanks to Him and praise His name."
I Thessalonians 5:18 (NT NIV)
"Give thanks in all circumstances, for this is God's will for you in Christ Jesus." Philippians 4:6 (N.T.NIV)
"Do not be anxious about anything, but in everything, by prayer and petition, with thanksgiving, present your requests to God."
I try to live by this verse every day.

My poem: "THANKFUL" 7-5-21

"We need to be thankful for everything God gives us, As we know each thing comes to teach us.
Every situation is there for a purpose, And our Lord has sent them so He can search us.

He wants to know how we'll handle things,
So all these situations he brings.

We need to keep praying,
So we know what He is saying.
We only need to thank Him for His results,
As He is in control and never bolts."

Has anyone ever asked you how far back in life can you remember? It's quite a mind exercise should you try to pick your brain. I actually can remember back to a time when I was standing in my crib at maybe or so, and my parents picking me up and taking me with them somewhere. Where it was I don't remember, but I know my folks never had babysitters for us and always took us with them wherever they went.

It was probably either to a friend's house or to our grandparents who lived in Lafayette, In. while we lived in Peoria, Il. which was a bit of a drive. I would have slept all the way there if that was where we were going. I don't remember arriving any where, but I do remember the thrill of being lifted out of my crib and being taken somewhere with my folks.

I also remember getting to take my naps on my parents' bed and my playing with my mother's jewelry box while I was supposed to be napping.

Another cool thing was my mother's fox stole that had a tail at one end and a head at the other. The head had a clip for a mouth and she would wear it around her neck with the mouth (clip) pinching the tail. I thought it was so cool, because it was real and I would pretend the fox was going to get all the bad people not that I knew any bad people. But it was a fun game.

Do you remember an embarrassing moment in your life? One would not suspect that a three or four year old could ever get embarrassed, but you better believe they can, and I know because it happened to me. It is still very vivid in my mind just 77 or 78 years later. I remember struggling in my mind to be sure to say something just right so that my folks WOULD NOT think I was dumb by saying the wrong thing. I knew when someone was very tired they might say. "Oh, I'm all in" or "I'm tired out." I wanted to say it just right, but when my dad sat me on the kitchen table after we had been to a school carnival, I carefully said a well-thought out statement of, "I'm all out." When they both laughed, I knew I had said it wrong. While they thought it was cute, all I wanted to do was crawl under the table and hide.

Now if you think that's not too bad, I'll tell you a story when I was about fourteen that really devastated me. A young teenage girl can really be scarred, especially if the embarrassment is in front of a young gentleman caller.

Remember back in the 50's when we girls wore lots of stiff crinolines and hoop skirts? One Spring early evening my male friend and I were going out-probably to the park since it was about six to eight blocks away. We approached the top of our stairway down to the sidewalk. There was no railing, and my skirt stuck out so far that I could not see the edge of the first step. I miss-stepped and fell head over heels all the way to the bottom with my skirts above my head. I was so embarrassed, that I jumped up without saying anything and ran back into the house. The poor fellow (Chuck) was left standing alone. I suspect he might have thought it funny, but I sure didn't. I think it was some time before we spoke again. To this day we are friends and I had never repeated that story until just the other day some seventy years later to his wife of all people. We both had a good laugh at that. Chuck may have been embarrassed as well, as he said nothing. If we can't laugh at ourselves, we are in a sad state. But a teenager is not as strong as an eighty year old.

Talk about memories, I have one more I remember when I was about three. I liked to sing and make up songs. My mother had just given me a bath and I was getting ready for bed. As I stood nude in front of the mirror, I sang "London Bridge is falling down, falling down, my BARE lady instead of my Fair lady." I thought I was so clever. I suppose it was since I was only three.

I have had a few things on my bucket list to do while I'm old but haven't given up yet. It may be hard to top what I did on my seventy-fifth birthday, because it was a bit daring but oh so fun.

I went with my twenty-four-year-old granddaughter skydiving. Many folks thought I was crazy, but we went tandem at a very safe reputable place in Frankfurt, In. We had both been wanting to, so we finally made the plans.

The next year I bought a bicycle and hadn't been on one for about thirty years. I had to buy a smaller one since my legs were so short cause I wanted to be able to touch the ground without having to get off.

The year after that I wanted to do something else I hadn't done for about thirty years. I went horseback riding with my daughter and granddaughter. I have one more thing I'd like to do that is daredevilish. I want to go up for a balloon flight. it can be dangerous, but sounds fun. Now I just have to find a good spot close by.

Gene and I took Corrine up for a balloon ride when she was younger, but it was pretty safe as it was tethered, so couldn't get too far away. Since I am over eighty, I probably should slow down a bit. I guess adventure is in my blood. It certainly was in Jeff's blood to be adventurous. He had been to about eighty countries, ridden a Yak, went bungy jumping and who knows what else. We both had jumped in freezing water after a hot sauna, and that is stimulating.

It's really very Scandinavian.

Leon & I had a four-seater Cessna plane at one time and we both learned to fly. He was much better at it than I was and he had gone across country and even learned to pilot a glider with no engine. I wasn't that brave.

The first flight we went on together after Lee got his pilot license was to Chicago to the little one strip airport by Navy Pier with water on three sides. I don't think it exists any more. We went up to meet and go to dinner with my brother and sister-in-law. The airport closed at midnight, so we had to hurry back before that happened in order to leave. We got there just a few minutes before the bewitching hour, and as we were taxiing out to take off, they turned of the lights and we couldn't see anything. They knew we were there and trying to take off, so I couldn't understand why they didn't wait until we were airborne. Crazy people! Luckily, Lee was pretty good at piloting And did a fantastic job getting us off the ground, but I don't think I've ever been so scared.

CHAPTER FOUR

WWII Time (1937-1945)

Matthew 24:6 (NIV)
"You will hear of wars and rumors of wars, but see to it you are not alarmed. Such things must happen, but the end is still to come."

Matthew 19:19 (NIV)
"Honor your father and your mother, and love your neighbor as yourself."

I know mankind has been involved in wars forever, but God still wants us to try to get along. People are basically the same the world over and it would be nice if we could love the world of peoples.

My Poem: "Neighbor"

"Revenge in the form of emotion or actions is bad.
So remember bearing a grudge will make folks mad.
We love ourselves as we've been taught,
So it can't be so hard to love a neighbor as we thought.
If we're taught love and forgiveness from the start,
We can practice it completely and not just in part.
God, our Father, loved us first-
And we're given so much of it-we feel like we could burst.
Jesus, His son, loved us too,
Now it's our turn to give some away where it is due."

By Marilyn Sandberg Grenat

Nostradamus had predicted a great deal of history's tragedies like the French Revolution, the great fire of Chicago, the building bombing of the twin tower sky scrapers in New York City and the beast of Germany (Hister-Hitler) who killed the six million Jews at Aushwitz seventy-six years ago. Hitler was a true beast to mankind. He predicted the three antichrists as Napoleon Bonaparte, Hister (or Hitler) with the third yet to come.

In 1937, Amelia Earhart was an entrepreneur that encouraged women at Purdue University to be individuals and to pursue their dreams with education and careers. She did just that for herself and decided to fly around the world with the help of the University President with a Lockheed aircraft. She sent back journals to her husband, George Palmer Putnam and they are in Purdue's archives today and her whereabouts are unknown. However, she still accomplished a lot for women and the flying exhibition.

I admired her so much that I gave my second daughter a middle name after Amelia.

Perfect moments can be had, but they can not be preserved.

Franklin D. Roosevelt died unexpectedly on April 12, 1945, and his Vice President, Harry Truman became the thirty-third president of the United States. On August 6, 1945, he approved the dropping of the Atom bomb on Hiroshima, Japan. Three days later on August 9, 1945, a bomb was dropped on Nagasaki, and Japan surrendered and on August 14, 1945, WWII was over. The very sad thing was that people were vaporized. Usually really bad things happen even to end other bad things.

His presidency did some good things as it saw the founding of the United Nations. He fought Communism with gusto. Truman was not always greatly liked or even appreciated, however, my father felt he was one of our greatest presidents.

In 1940, during my birth year, the movie, "Gone with the Wind" took a lot of Oscars.

Bob Hope hosted Oscars for several years and "Thanks for the Memory" became his song.

The Academy Awards were known at his house as Passover, as he never got any Oscar Awards himself. He said he had a speech in his pocket for the last fourteen years just in case.

Bob Hope had entertained the troops overseas for many years as a selfless contribution. In 1964 he and Connie Stevens entertained to troops in Saigon, Viet-Nam. He asked Connie to sing something and she sang "Silent Night" to them and said their families would love to be here with you-then the troops joined in the singing. This was a tear jerker.

In 1991 Bob gave his last performance to the USO show for the troops.

During the war there were lots of scarcities. Women had a hard time getting nylon hose, so they made silk hose. Europe, as well, had shortages of many things. We had problems getting sugar, coffee, butter, and more I'm sure. Since I was so young, I didn't know all of them. I remember they started making margarine and a big one-pound block of white stuff looked like lard, but was margarine. They had an orange liquid capsule with it and we were supposed to mix it in that block, so it would look like butter. That was always my job to do. We received ration coupons for things, and I remember my folks sending sugar, coffee, and silk hose to Sweden to our relatives during that time.

CHAPTER FIVE

Starting a Different Foreign Life (1946-1947)

I Peter 3:8-9 "Finally, all of you, live in harmony with one another; be sympathetic, love as brothers, be compassionate and humble. 9 Do not repay evil with evil or insult with insult."

Galatians 6:10 "Therefore, as we have opportunity, let us do good to all people, especially to those who belong to the family of believers."

My Poem: "Opportunity" By Marilyn Sandberg Grenat

"We should always be kind to others,
Especially to those close to us like brothers.
They can be our biological family, our church family,
Or our circle of friends.
But also make all outsiders feel
Like we care and welcome them like a deal!
Never pass an opportunity to show graciousness,
As we can do this with expansive spaciousness."

This brings me to the remembrance of an experience my brother and I had when my father and mother picked us up lock, stock and trunk, so to speak, and moved us to a foreign country.

My mother had to be humble & compassionate in a foreign country that thought she might be a spoiled American woman that didn't know how to cope with a possible hard life on the farm where Grandpa (Farfar's) home was very primitive. She was a hard worker and determined to show them her strength and capabilities. She learned on her own and proved them all wrong. They soon learned to love and respect her even though no one was willing to teach her these primitive ways. She learned to split wood, haul in water from the well, start a wood-burning fire in the stove and bake with no thermometer. She was soon admired and loved and respected.

By the time 1946 rolled around, Leonard decided he wanted to take his whole family to Sweden for a trip to meet his family.

Leonard had just completed eleven years at Caterpillar in Peoria, Illinois. He was going to do some consultant work in Sweden for them too.

I remember mother sitting at the furnace door chucking our school papers and drawings in with tears streaming down her face in remorse. She knew we couldn't take everything with us, so had to down-size. I remember a few of her treasured things she chose to take were her miniature Singer sewing machine which actually came in very handy. She took her beautifully hand-tooled leather envelope purse, and her much-needed full-length fur coat as it got very cold in Sweden.

They packed up their belongings, sold their house on Armstrong and were off to Sweden on the Swedish-American line MS Drottningholm.

We had big trunks to put our belongings in and it was fascinating watching them derrick-lift them down into the hold of the ship. The cargo deck of the ship held many treasures. One could only hope all came to destination in good shape. Ours seemed to do just that.

Aunt Veva & Uncle Steve drove us to New York to catch the ship that took us to Gothenburg (Goteborg) the ten long days. Poor mother was so seasick and hardly could eat anything, so lost lots of weight on the trip. The rest of us faired just fine.

However, one morning as it was especially rough, I woke up and said, "I don't like how this boat hops!" Poor mom spent most of her time in bed below in the cabin.

It could be fun or very trying. My brother Ralph did not have a very easy time in the one room school house in my dad's village of Haurida. There were two one-room school houses.

Ralph's was fourth grade to sixth grades, and he had a fairly nasty school master who gave him a very hard time and instructed the older boys to be mean to him as well. He did not like foreigners-especially Americans I presume. With the foreign language also being difficult for Ralph, it was an especially difficult time for him. The girls, however, were kind to him. When our Dad found out about this nastiness, he went straight to school to confront the school master and to set him straight. He said, "Ralph is as Swedish as you and I, born of two Swedes.

In fact, I am originally from this village myself, and will not tolerate your treating him in this fashion." The instructor did begin to be a bit better, but always seemed to have it in for poor Ralph.

Ralph flourished anyway and learned the language and never lost out that year he was away from his American school.

Marilyn, on the other hand, had a lovely teacher by the name Betty Berring, in the one room school house for first-third graders. She treated Marilyn very well and even knew a little English. Since Swedish children didn't go to kindergarten and didn't start first grade until they were seven, everyone wondered if Marilyn would be Okay at age six to go to a foreign school. Not only was she one year younger than the rest, but she was pretty small for her age anyway. Miss (Froken) Berring helped Marilyn a great deal and even catered a bit to her.

I remember when we came in from the cold, she even set me on the warm stove to warm up. Marilyn actually did just fine in her new foreign school. Children normally do very well at learning a foreign language when they are quite young-especially if they are thrown in with people that speak nothing but that language. Miss Berring and mother told me I did quite well and never had to take first grade over when we got back to the United States as they thought might happen previously.

They have a beautiful fancy cursive penmanship in Sweden and they even taught it as early as first grade. It was really fun practicing that fancy writing. And to think they don't want to teach cursive writing here in the States anymore. It's an artform and I would be saddened to see it stop.

My math was quite different too, and I remember using an abacus for counting, etc. I remember my father telling me they taught him algebra in fifth grade when he was in school there.

They don't teach it here until high school. No wonder our European and other foreign countries are so far ahead of us.

My mother used my grandmother's old coat to cut up and make me a warm winter coat with her trusty little Singer sewing machine. She was a proficient seamstress.

We had no indoor plumbing at Farfar's country house, which meant, of course, we only had an outhouse for toileting, with pots under the beds that we had to empty every morning. The outhouse was about a block away, and it seemed far when the snow was deep and air was so cold. It was a two-holer with a large catalogue for toilet paper.

My mother luckily knew Swedish as she had heard sermons in Swedish as a youngster and had taken her confirmation in Swedish from a Swedish-speaking minister in Lafayette at the Swedish Mission Covenant church.

She knew how to bake good Swedish Limpa rye bread, which was a necessary staple in a Swedish home. She was used to her nice gas stove in the States, so she had to teach herself how to adjust to bake in a wood-burning stove. It was a whole new ballgame for sure. There was nothing lazy about my mother and she surprised and pleased them all.

We experienced all the traditions with "Dop I Gryttan" (dip in the pot), real candles on the tree, many more Christmas pastries and delicacies', Ost kaka, Pankaka, sill (pickled herring), medvorst (salami), rice pudding, sylta (head cheese made from a pig's head), blood pudding and so much more with farmer's cheese and at least seven kinds of cookies and a torta (cake with yummy fruit filling along with fruit soup and whipped cream.

They always hung a lit star in the window instead of the lit tree.

If there was room, the tree would be in the middle of the room, so all could dance around it. We always went to the woods to choose our special Christmas tree and would chop it down and haul it home and put it up the night before Christmas Eve when we would celebrate Christmas together. Christmas morning we would go at six AM to the church for Jullotta (Christmas Service).

After Christmas we would put the tree in the yard and tie pieces of bread on the branches for the birds and then take the trees to the center of town on January 13th on King Knut's birthday to burn them in one big bonfire.

My cousin, Maj-Britt was very special and loved Christmas. She would always create a poem and attach it to each of her Christmas packages. It was clever and fun to hear folks read them.

My folks, Leonard and second wife, Anna, and I decided in 1992 that we missed the Swedish Christmases and would like to go to Sweden one more time, so we went and enjoyed it very much until my father had a heart attack on Christmas Eve-one day before we were going to go back home to the U.S.A. It was devastating, as he and Anna had to stay another six weeks before the doctor would let him go home.

When we were in Sweden in 1946-47, Ralph and I got to ski to school in the wintertime. Since I was so little, a local man carved my small skis to fit me. We had fun waxing them to make them go faster.

Our family had fun riding on a sparkster, which was a chair-like seat on runners (skis). Mom would sit on the seat with me in her lap and Ralph and dad would stand behind on the runners and dad would kick start us and we would go sailing down the hill lickety-split. It was great fun. I haven't seen one in years, but I think they still make them, as I have seen them advertised in catalogues. One would have to have a lot of snow and hope they wouldn't plow the roads to use them or just stay on snowy hills.

When we got back to the States, my Swedish Aunt Veva and Uncle Steve were tickled pink to hear Ralph and me speaking Swedish so fluently.

Sadly enough, the folks rarely spoke it at home, so we soon lost it. That was sad, because I hated losing that capability. We only went to Sweden every seven-fifteen years and it was hard to pick it up fluently again when we'd only stay for a short time. I went more than Ralph though and would try in 1954 at age fourteen to pick up a bit more. I asked daddy lots of questions about what the relatives said and how do I say this or that. It was important to me to learn again. We were there then about four months and I was able to pick up a bit more.

I went again in 1960 after graduating from North Park College in Chicago, which was our Denominational school with a Swedish background. I took two years of Swedish there and learned to read, write and spell it better. I kept up with my writing letters in Swedish to my Swedish cousins that didn't know English. The young people did better as they were required to take six years of English in school. However, book learning is not the same as being in the country hearing nothing but that language from the natives. That's the best way to learn a foreign tongue by any measure.

I have no one to practice it with, but I try to keep it up on my own and practice it by myself with pretend conversations with myself and then answer myself in the same manner. My cousins seem to think I do pretty well considering I have no one to practice with. I do have a professor cousin in Lund, Sweden who speaks very proficient English and I never have to speak Swedish with him.

It is quite fun being a polyglot. Knowing more than one language-even as a bilingual it keeps one's mind always working if you practice in conversing, writing, and reading the second language. I may only go to Sweden every five to fifteen years, but I always try to keep up those skills and keep learning. My "Swedish/English Lexicon" is always close at hand ready to learn a new word or two. A polyglot can even blend the two languages in the same sentence at which my father was very proficient. He did what we Swedes call blanda ihop (blended together). He would mix Swedish words with English words in the same sentence.

It brought a few laughs a few times from folks on both sides of the pond. When I do this, my youngest daughter gets mad at me.

She always says, "Mom, you know I don't understand Swedish." I always tell her it's never too late to learn. You need to listen, ask questions and try to repeat-that is if you WANT to learn. While I always try to be frugal, I am careful not to be parsimonious, being overly restrained from spending some extra money to enjoy some happiness. I saved carefully for several years to take and enjoy one last trip to Sweden with my middle daughter, Kristina. She had been the only one of my four children who had not been to Sweden to see and experience our heritage. I felt it was her turn. These tickets had been purchased eight months prior to when we were to go in 2020, and then the covid pandemic hit and we were not able to go then.

Now we have repurchased the tickets and are scheduled to go for Midsummer in June of 2022. This time it was a go. I wrote a Swedish/English dictionary for her of often used phrases and terms that I thought she might need to use, but I don't think she's even looked at it much less tried to learn any of it. One has to really be interested in wanting to learn a foreign language. We so enjoyed our Midsummer Fest trip in June 2022.

When we were in Sweden as youngsters, Ralph loved to ski and venture out in the woods around our grandpa's homestead. One day he did just that, but being in the middle of a dark forest, everything can be confusing and look the same. After he had been out all day and seemed to be lost, he felt he needed to strategize how to get home safely. As the sun started to go down, he figured out which way was North and he went that direction until he found a fence and followed the road home. The folks were glad to see him arriving, and he was happy to have made it finally.

While we were in Sweden I had a little kitten I named after the wild flowers that bloomed in the woods-"Sippa". She was a little gray tiger-marked cat and very smart. She would always be waiting for me at the end of the lane at the same time I would be coming home from school. It was like she had an inner-clock. One day we went to a funeral in the car about two miles away, and when we came out of there, she was waiting for us by our car. How in the world could she possibly have known where we were going? It's almost like a "Lassie" story of the smart dog.

One day she was bitten by some animal and she came home with a big hole in her side.

She came up to my mother, who she must have felt was her protector, and laid down at her feet and meowed mournfully. Mother said, "Ralph, are you tormenting your sister's cat again?" He said, "No, Mother, I haven't touched her." When mother examined her, she discovered the wound. Mother tried to clean it as best she could, but cats and dogs have healing properties in their saliva, and she licked it together and healed herself.

One day when all the snow melted and made a big pond in the woods, my brother picked Sippa up by the tail and flung her out into the middle of the pond. I guess cats do have nine lives, as she swam right back to me.

She did do one dumb, but funny thing though. We had a birdfeeder outside our kitchen window and she used to love to sit on the back of the kitchen sofa and watch them. She would forget there was a window there and lunge for them and invariably hit her head on the window. Poor kitty. I loved her so much that it broke my heart when we went back to the States and I had to leave her.

Our time in Sweden was a wonderful learning experience where we met relatives and made new friends. My best friend was a little girl from Finland named Perico.

We were the only foreigners in our first grade classroom. Since Sweden was neutral during the war and Finland was not, many Finnish families sent their children to live in Sweden with Swedish families as foster parents. She was still there the next year after the war was over.

I had one of my cousins take in a Finnish girl and they ended up adopting her and she stayed.

Many went home, but some stayed and integrated into the Swedish culture.

I will always be grateful for my early Swedish experience, but there was one thing I hated. The girls had to wear long tan cotton stockings in the winter, like hose with garters on our panties. They were such a nuisance. It reminded me of Pippi Long Stockings in the book. If they had been like leotards it might have been more comfortable, but they weren't invented yet.

In 1947 we headed for Gothenburg to catch our ship home. We arrived in New York City in the Spring and after visiting with dad's friend Bror and his wife Elsie who lived in Brooklyn, we headed for Lafayette, Indiana, where my other Grandpa (Mother's dad), Algot Swanson, lived. We stayed a few days with him until my folks bought a two-story house two blocks away on Center Street.

Chapter Five- Marilyn & Ralph going to school in Haurida 1946

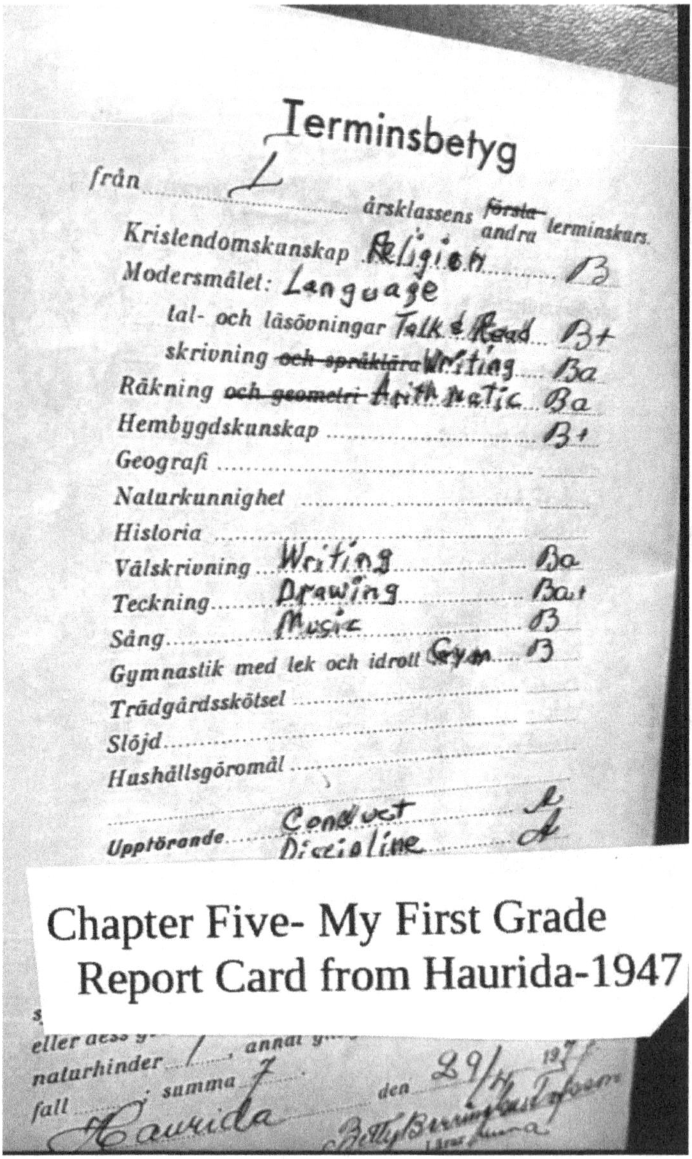

Terminsbetyg

från 1 årsklassens ~~första~~ andra terminskurs

Kristendomskunskap Religion B

Modersmålet: Language

tal- och läsövningar Talk & Read B+

skrivning ~~och språklära~~ Writing Ba

Räkning ~~och geometri~~ Arithmatic Ba

Hembygdskunskap B+

Geografi

Naturkunnighet

Historia

Välskrivning Writing Ba

Teckning Drawing Ba+

Sång Music B

Gymnastik med lek och idrott Gym B

Trädgårdsskötsel

Slöjd

Hushållsgöromål

Conduct A

Uppförande Discipline A

eller dess ... annat ...

naturhinder 1

fall ... summa 7 den 29/4 1947

Haurida Betty Berring ...

lärarinna

Chapter Five- My First Grade Report Card from Haurida-1947

The snow really could
get that deep in Sweden
MELTING SNOW
FORMS A LAKE
WOODS

Chapter Five ~~Ships~~
To Sweden 1946
MS Gripsholm
From-Sweden-1947
MS Drottningholm
DROTTNINGHOLM FROM SWEDEN TO USA
IN 1947
CHAPTER 5

CHAPTER SIX

The 1950's

Philippians 3:14 (NIV) "I press on toward the goal to win the prize for which God has called me to heavenward in Christ Jesus."

I am always trying to seek God's will for me, as I know whatever He has in mind for me would be far greater than anything I could imagine for myself. While we know He is in control, we somehow have a problem in turning everything over to Him and His guidance. We like being in control of our own destiny even if it might not be what God wants for us- even if it's bad for us.

Jeremiah 29:11 (NIV) "For I know the plans I have for you, declares the Lord, 'plans to prosper you and not to harm you, plans to give you hope and a future."

Ephesians 3:20 & 21 (NIV) "Now to him who is able to do immeasurably more than all we ask or imagine, according to His power that is at work within us, 21 to him be glory in the church and in Christ Jesus through out all generations, for ever and ever! Amen.

My Poem "The Spirit Leads Me" written January 7, 2018 by Marilyn Sandberg Grenat

"I Corinthians twelve
Teaches us where we should delve.

We each have special gifts
And to us they give substantial lifts.

God has put us here
And it's all very clear.

The Holy Spirit has purpose for us
And to that we should realize
That in the end it's a real prize.

Both for us giving
And to the person living,

To receive and be blessed
By all the best.
God and we have to offer.

While we knowledge receive,
Of where God wants us, we must believe

That it is Him to all glory be given.
That is the reason for our liven.

The Holy Spirit was given to direct us,
And by His guiding, it's a plus.

Lord, make me pure in heart-
Never from you to depart."

By 1950 I was ten and went to fifth grade at Ford School which was soon on it's way out. It's location was at fourteenth and South Streets. It had been built between 1907-1915 and the Army reserve built an 18,000 square foot building there on that spot in 1976. It is now the Lafayette Police Department training building. The new school, Murdock School in Murdock Park was built in 1951 where I attended sixth grade under the tutelage of Mr. Hanley Breedon. Seventh grade was attended at

Durgan School on S. 18th. Street, eighth was attended at Washington in 1953 and high school was attended at Jefferson High School downtown from 1954-1958 at Brown and ninth streets. I spent 1958-1960 at our denominational college at North Park College in Chicago, Illinois. I graduated with an Associate of Arts degree in Liberal Arts. It was their last year for the two-year degree and the first year for their four year degree program. They are now considered a University and they also have a Seminary department where ministers are ordained and missionaries train. It is a very fine religious school and they have many students representing many different countries with "Student Abroad" programs to other countries as well as them at North Park.

In May, 1989 I graduated with a certification of Paralegal Studies from Indiana Paralegal Law Institute in Lafayette, Indiana. I have been able to help a few folks pro bono with a few legal documents as well as myself.

I learned my Swedish quite well at age six in 1946. I can attest to the fact that living amongst the people and being young is the best way to learn a foreign language. However, if you are taken out of that environment and don't use or hear it any more, you can forget it pretty quickly too. Even though my folks knew Swedish, they didn't use it much at home unless it was a brief comment to try to keep information from us kids. One has to be interested in keeping it up, ask questions, pay attention, and ask how to say something and then practice it. We perhaps only went to Sweden every eight to fifteen years, so we only got to observe and practice it then for short periods.

I finally took Swedish in college for two years since our school had a Swedish background where I learned to read, write and spell it. As you may know, it's difficult to learn much of a foreign language in a classroom situation. However, I was very interested, paid better attention and truly tried to learn enough to use these scattered times we went.

By 1960, I really did learn a bit more. If I didn't remember something, I would check my SwedishAmerican dictionary (Lexicon) to try to spell and say things correctly. I continued to write letters in Swedish to my Swedish cousins so I would keep in practice. I would also call them on the phone and try to talk to them. To start out, I would write it down before calling them or writing to them so I wouldn't look or sound so dumb in using improper Swedish grammar. They were very forgiving if I made mistakes because I was making a bigger effort than some of them who hadn't learned much English. The younger people do better now as they had to take six years of English in school. I have a professor cousin who speaks perfect English, so I never have to speak Swedish to him. Over the years, I have built up my vocabulary.

My son, Jeff went to North Park University as well and even spent one semester at a college in Sweden as a student abroad. He had a successful business he started as an event planner and had been to eighty countries in his travels helping CEOs from Fortune 500 companies.

My three girls all succeeded in their education and work ethics as well. My two oldest girls became Dental Hygienists and my youngest had her own nail business for about ten years and then spent about twenty years as a successful title closer with several different title companies and now works in an office for a builder, which she loves.

In the 1950's I was ten to nineteen and this took me into my growing up years in Lafayette, Indiana including my teenage years. I loved growing up in this medium-small town. Purdue University was just across the Wabash River, so it made our town seem bigger and not so much of a hick town. After all, the University brought class, education, entertainment, and many different nationalities. This is a very well-thought-of University with a variety of classes. Most of our astronauts have been educated at PU, and we have nursing, architects, engineers, and agricultural studies as well. People have come from all over the world to be educated there. I was once on the board at the International Center near the University and was in charge of finding American families to host some of International students to teach them American ways in their homes and the community. It was rewarding to match the folks up with the students. We wanted them to feel at home in a foreign country.

Annette, my oldest, and her first husband, attended some classes there and Kristina took some classes there as well. Jeff wanted a smaller school, so he chose my alma mater at North Park College (now University) in Chicago, Ill. to attend. I worked at Purdue University for sixteen years in Accounting.

Ralph and I both attended Jefferson High School and North Park College. Our grades were three years apart, but we both were in our church Hi-League youth group together and had many of the same teenage friends. It was a nice mix of ages. We have remained friends with some of them to this day.

Phil and Sandy Denhardt and Chuck still go to our church, so I see them when we're all there.

Now that we're in our twilight years, many have gone to be with the Lord, but we'll see them again some day in our heavenly realm.

Our tremendous youth and main pastor was Norbert Johnson, when we were teenagers. He and his lovely wife, Elaine, came to us when he was fresh out of seminary. They are now both gone. They lived across the street at first from us in the parsonage just three blocks from the Evangelical Covenant church at 16th and Grove streets. I babysat their three children.

We built two more new churches that we kept outgrowing. Both of them have been on Ninth street. I saw our congregation grow from thirty-five members in 1947 to over three hundred and fifty today. I have seen several ministers come and go over the past seventy-four years as well.

The Scandinavian fairy tales talked about ugly trolls with long noses and furry tails that lived in the woods. When I was little, and played in the woods, I was always afraid they were going to jump out from behind a tree and scare me. Remember the story of the troll that lived under the bridge and wouldn't let anyone pass over his bridge? Well, even though it's just a myth, I was still scared of them. The uglier they are, the cuter they are to me today.

I love them now. I wanted to buy a replica of one when I was in Sweden in 2013. Jeff and I searched every gift shop and couldn't find one until we got to the Stockholm Airport gift shop.

Even though I thought they were too expensive, Jeff said, "Mom you've been wanting one, so I will buy it for your birthday." Bless his heart! Especially since he is gone now, I treasure it even more.

Pastor Johnson had a wonderful two-year Confirmation class for us from 1952-1954. He was a very tough teacher, but he taught us a lot. We had to memorize a lot of scripture and catechism. We had to know it all, because we didn't know which questions he was going to ask us in front of the whole congregation. We had to write a long speech and give it in front of the whole church too. It was a good experience for us, but we were so nervous and didn't want to mess up in front of every body. It was almost like being in college.

Our whole youth group came the farthest distance to our Covenant Harbor Bible Camp at Lake Geneva, Wisconsin and we all got gold

Purdue hats to wear, so folks would know we all belonged together. It was quite fun. My Senior year in 1958 while Leon and I were going together we went to camp and the last night was the big dinner where a King and Queen were chosen to reign at the dinner. Leon and I were chosen by the camp to be the King and Queen. It was really exciting. We got a picture of it too.

In the 1950's Pizza got to be very popular, and a big Pizza parlor was built on the West Side and it was called Bruno's. All the young folks liked to go there, and when we didn't go there, everyone came to our house, as my Mom started making the teens pizza.

Bruno's was a family-run restaurant and they stayed in business for many years and only recently closed it down as the family felt they got too old to run it anymore. it was a main stay for many years. They use it for catering & special parties now.

Mom not only always had the door open to teenagers, but she welcomed many folks. Her door was always open for church members, friends and relatives. She always found room for anyone who needed a place to stay.

Colossians 4:5 (NIV) "Be wise in the way you act toward outsiders; make the most of every opportunity."

I babysat quite a bit for the neighbors. Not only for the Pastors kids but for the Osborn girls as well who lived next door to the Pastor. They also went to our church as several of our neighbors did. We were all a friendly neighborhood.

By the time I was in high school, (1954-1958) I started working all four years at the local library as a page after school. My folks bought a restaurant and filling station in 1953 at Highway 52 & South streets called the White Cottage. I worked as hard as any adult helping my mom in the kitchen and waiting tables. My dad only paid me thirty-five cents an hour, but that's all I was making baby-sitting too. My brother was seventeen and he helped my dad pumping gas and washing car windows. The folks made a profit when they sold it in 1954, and that is when my dad and I went to Sweden for four months. My principal thought my trip would be more educational than staying in school for the last two months, so I just had to do some extra homework before I left. With all that settled, I was set to pack my trunk for our voyage on the "Stockholm" Swedish/American line ship going from New York City, New York to Gothenburg, Sweden in April, 1954.

It was so fascinating watching them derrick-lift those trunks down into the hold in the ship that carried the luggage. Sometimes they would even drop one and I would say, "I hope there's nothing breakable in there." This reminded me on the way home to be sure to pack my dad's beautiful childhood oil lamp in heavy sweaters and a blanket to protect it from breakage. The frail thin glass chimney was very fragile, so I packed wood shavings in it. It was a special heirloom that my dad had studied by as a child. Dad enjoyed it for awhile, and then I enjoyed it, and then Jeff got to enjoy it last. Unfortunately, it got broken in a recent move, but now we can enjoy the pictures and memories of it.

In fact I learned many things that summer! I became a pioneer woman like my mother did in 1946. I wouldn't trade that summer for anything. Grandpa was glad to see us, but nothing had changed in his primitive living conditions. There was still no running water or indoor bathroom. The outhouse was still there in all it's glory! We still had to split wood for the wood-burning stove and haul water in and out to the smoke house to heat for the washtub in the yard and wash cloths on the scrub board. It was quite an education for me. I still had to ride Grandpa (Farfar's) bike to the next farm for milk too. At least the cows didn't mind my singing as I rode by the meadow.

I even got my first heartbreak from a handsome young German boy I met on the ship going over. He worked on the ship and was three years my senior with beautiful dark brown curly hair, named Willy. I was devastated that he never wrote to me like he promised.

Dad bought an old Model T car and we traveled around to visit relatives and every time we'd come into a town, I'd be so embarrassed and hide on the floor of the car. I'd give my eye teeth for one of those now as long it would run.

It was a treat to go into Huskvarna to see my Aunt Helfrid and Uncle Sven, as they had a modern kitchen with electric appliances, running water and an indoor bathroom with a shower. They had a nice corner yard where we had lots of coffee parties and she had a lot of fruit and vegetables and pretty flowers in her yard.

Jim Mills, Ralph's buddy, and Ralph met us in New York.

Dad bought a beautiful coffee set and brought home to Mother, and I am enjoying it today.

I will always treasure that special time I had with my daddy and my Swedish relatives. I'm always grateful for the opportunity to learn more proper Swedish language.

When we got home I started high school, and went all four years to Jefferson High School downtown on 9th. Street in Lafayette, Indiana. Then in the Fall of 1958, I went off to college in Chicago, Illinois to our denominational school, North Park College. I graduated in two years, as it was a Junior College transitioning into a four-year school. I got my Associate of Arts degree in 1960 in Liberal Arts.

Then in 1989 I got another Associate Arts degree in Paralegal studies at Indiana Paralegal Law Institute.

I learned my Swedish quite well at age six in 1946 I can attest to the fact that living amongst the people and being young is the best way to learn a foreign language. However, if you are taken out of that environment and don't use or hear it anymore, you can soon forget it. My folks did not speak it after we got back home, so we soon forgot it. Since we only went to Sweden every seven years in college and asked my dad a lot of questions about Swedish in 1954 when we were visiting there for four months. One has to be interested and want to learn and ask lots of questions as to what was said and how to say something. I keep tit up now as I practice it with myself. I learned to read, write, and speak it again after I had been to college and my seven trips back t Sweden. I don't ever want to lose it again. My cousins in Sweden are very encouraging and say they are amazed at how I can speak so much Swedish now. The young people there have to take six years of English so they do very well t speaking to us and understanding, but folks my age won't speak much English. I do, however, have a Swedish cousin just a little it younger than me who speaks perfect English. H e was a professor at Lund University, so I never have to speak Swedish to him.

White Cottage Restaurant
& Standard Filling Station
at South St. & 52 By-Pass
1953-54-Where I first worked
at age 13 for my mom & dad.

~~Chapter Six MS Stockholm~~
Ship to Sweden with Dad 1954

Chapter Six Primitive
Wash on the scrubboard
1954

Chapter Six – Sandberg Family 1955
Marilyn-15, Ralph-18

Chapter Six - Mom's Pizza 1955

Chapter Six – King Lee & Queen Marilyn of Covenant Harbor Bible Camp- 1958

Graduation trip to
Sweden-1960
Rose from Aunt Helfrid's
Garden

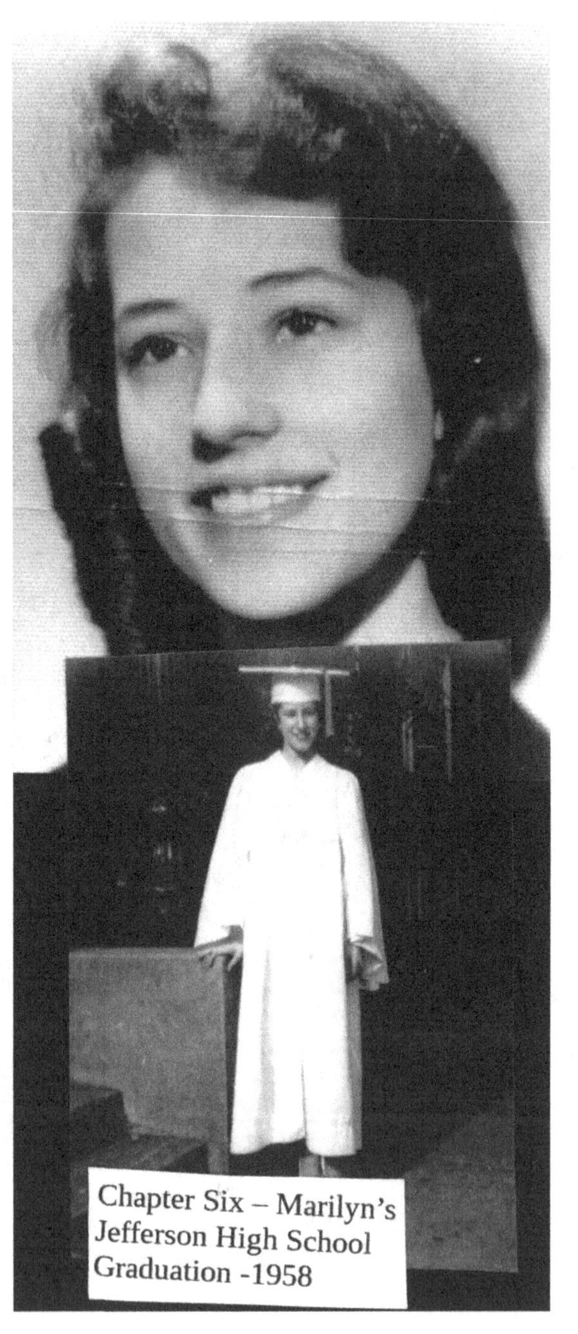

Chapter Six – Marilyn's Jefferson High School Graduation -1958

My Graduation
Dad-me-Mom
1958-1960

CHAPTER SEVEN

Our Swedish Trips (1954, 1960, 1975,1992, 2013, & 2022)

The Lord will protect us always even in our travels. Psalm 91:9-11 (NIV) 9 "If you make the Most High your dwelling—even the Lord, who is my refuge—10 then no harm will befall you, no disaster will come near your dwelling. 11 For He will command His angels concerning you to guard you in all your ways." Psalm 91:14 b "I will protect him, for he acknowledges my name."

My Poem "Protection" November 7, 2021.
By Marilyn Sandberg Grenat

"The most comforting thought is knowing our Savior always looks out for us.
To His children it is a definite plus.

It matters not wherever we may be.
This brings us peaceful glee.

He protects us when we sleep,
As we know this promise He will keep.

He protects us as we work or go to school,
And this is admirably cool.

He protects us when we play or go about,
As this is amazing wherever our route.

When we travel by sea or sky, by foot or by road,
He carefully looks after us we are told.

Wherever we are, we are protected and loved,
And this He does completely from above."

I already told you about our first trip in 1946 in Chapter Five, so I'll continue with my dad and my trip in 1954. He originally wanted to take my brother, Ralph, with him, but he didn't want to leave his girlfriend for the summer. Dad and I were gone for four months from April to July.

We had had the White Cottage Restaurant and filling station for about a year and due to our hard work, we were able to make a profit on it, but the folks felt like it was time to sell in the Spring of 1954. Mother was able to keep dad's Sandberg Engineering Manufacturer's business going while we were gone, plus she got a secretarial job working for the crew that was building the new Water-Waste Plant for the city of Lafayette. She and Ralph kept the home fires burning while dad and I were gone.

I learned so much that summer, and then I understood partially what my mother experienced when we first went in 1946. As I mentioned, she was very much like a pioneer woman learning how to split wood, build a fire in a wood-burning stove and how to bake bread and many other foods in such an old-fashioned contraption. We both learned how to cope with no indoor bathroom facilities nor running water. The well became another one of our obstacles.

I also learned how to put up hay to dry, how to plant and harvest potatoes, and how to draw, warm and carry water to a wash pail in the yard where I did our wash by hand on a scrub board and some times had to hurry to switch the still wet wash to a clothes line on the porch if a quick rain came up. There was no driving to the grocery store for milk!

It meant getting on Grandpa's much too big bicycle with the milk pail to go to the next farm to pick up a liter of fresh milk from the farmer's cow. I didn't mind so much, as it took me past pretty pastures & woods and I could sing on the way. Sometimes I would stop in the meadow so I could sing at the top of my lungs all the popular songs of 1954. The cows didn't seem to mind. Since I was very shy, I never wanted anyone else to hear me. My cousin was a band leader and he sometimes would ask me to come and sing with his band. Even though I really wanted to, I just couldn't bring myself to do it.

I got a little chicken when I first came and loved watching it grow. The most exciting thing about it, was that a couple of days before we were going to leave, this chicken laid it's first egg. I was thrilled to pieces. I had never lived on a farm, so this was all new to me at thirteen.

We would go into town in Huskvarna and Jonkoping to see Aunts & Uncles and many cousins, which was really fun as well. They had indoor plumbing! Hallelujah! I had some cousins, Maj Britt and Conrad, who had kids (my second cousins) that were close to my age. Conrad was the band leader, but he also had a photography store where he took lots of photographs. Later on when he built his new house, he made the basement entrance tall enough to accommodate huge trucks coming in with furniture where he photographed furniture for a catalogue. I would help his wife sometimes set up for the shots. It was pretty cool.

All of my Swedish cousins were pretty cool. One of them, who was the daughter of Aunt (Faster) Helfrid who was my dad's older sister was a nurse and also taught nursing. She seemed to always be going to school herself. Her name was Gullan and she had one sister named Ingrid. I thought she was so pretty and very progressive for that era, as she wore bright red nail polish and I had never seen anyone any where do that before. Faster Helfrid and Farbror (uncle-father's brother-in-law) Sven lived in Huskvarna and Uncle Sven worked at the Huskvarna factory down the hill from their house. We always had such fun with them and Annette and Jeff, my two oldest got to meet them in 1975. Gullan was quite a bit older than me, and she called me her little cousin. She knit me a pretty little yellow dress when I was six that looked like it was double-breasted with four big white buttons and a white collar and cuffs. I loved that dress. She also bought me a pretty turquoise flower enameled necklace that I love later. But most of all, I truly treasure my Swedish enameled blue and gold royalty pin that she got me; it has three Swedish gold crowns on a blue background. I wear it when I want to feel and dress Swedish.

In 1960 after I graduated from North Park College, my folks took me to Sweden on another fun trip. Since the countries were as close as states are to each other, I suggested we should visit some other countries while we were there. I said we've never done that and since dad has a car, I think we should go to a few places. We ended up going to Denmark, Norway, The Netherlands, Holland, Germany, France, and Belgium. Some of our experiences were delightful, while others were disturbing.

As I collectively think about our experience in France and my son's experience there forty years later, I don't feel like I'd ever like to go back. When we were there in 1960, my father had a headache and went to a drugstore to see if he could get some aspirin. Most European countries have some one in their stores who understand English, but it was funny we could never find ANYONE ANYWHERE that could understand us. Mother and I had waited in the car for him and he was gone a very long time, so I decided to look for him. When I found him struggling, I showed my frustration and pointed to his head and the row of pills. They seemed to get it right away. I think they were messing with him because he was older and American.

They do not like Americans. When I asked where the Eiffel Tower was from someone else, they shook their heads. I repeated again and they finally said, "Oh, I..Fell". Yeah, you're going to fall alright. Don't tell me they haven't heard that question from millions of tourists before. They were just enjoying messing with us, I do believe.

When my son was working there in about 2000, he was standing on a street corner waiting to cross at the light. My sister-in-law and her granddaughter were with him. We know the French like to kickbox. Because Jeff was American, we believe just out of orneriness and because of the fact that Jeff was American the Frenchman just up for no other reason kickboxed Jeff extremely hard in the upper part of his leg. It's a wonder he didn't brake a bone. Jeff was furious and ready to fight him, but Aunt Kathy talked him out of it, as she said, "We are in a foreign country and the police would be quick to put a foreigner in jail for disturbing the peace." So he left it alone, but he hurt for a couple of weeks and was bruised all the way from the hip to down past his knee.

In Norway we saw some of the most beautiful fjords and waterways. The Netherlands had gorgeous waterways with scenic little walking bridges. Holland had majestic windmills. My mother and I loved sweet licorice in America, so we got excited when we saw licorice in a candy store window with licorice in Belgium, so we went in to buy some. It was the biggest disappointment you can imagine, as it was very bitter! A hotel room in Belgium was a delightful surprise with a chandelier that sparkled in the middle of the room. We also were surprised to hear of the owner telling how much they liked the Americans and even was proud to show where a bullet was embedded in the woodwork from the war.

When we went to a bed and breakfast room that was over a bar in Germany, we were surprised to see young teenagers being served beer.

In Denmark we were thrilled to see the mermaid statue on the rock out in the bay, but sort of flabbergasted at seeing a middle-aged woman in an elevator smoking a great big fat cigar.

These are just a few of the things that stood out to us in European countries, and that I can still remember.

In 1975, it was my two oldest-Annette and Jeff that I took to Sweden for about three weeks. The two youngest were really too young to enjoy such a trip. Kristina was four and she stayed with her dad, Aunt Kathy and Uncle Ralph and a little bit with her godparents, Shirley and Jerry Maitlen, while Jennifer at two stayed with Grandma and Grandpa Sandberg. We were there during Midsummer time and they got such a kick out of the tradition of dancing around the Midsummer pole and singing "Sma Gradarna" (Small Frogs) that Maj-Britt taught them. They even wanted a midsummer pole at home the next summer after we had been there. We were all enthralled with the wooden giant just outside of Huskvarna. Jeff was really taken by it and wanted his picture of it with him posing beside it with arms crossed. When we went again in 2013, he wanted that same posed picture just thirty-eight years later. That picture was one on his funeral poster.

I was thrilled that the kids were excited about the trip and even got to meet my first grade teacher who was still living.

My father's friend Bror Wannerstrom's brother, Phillip and his wife Ruth still lived in the Haurida village where they all grew up. Their house was on the same property that their folks had lived in. Since they had passed, the house was empty, so we rented it for the time we were there. I had rented a car so I could get back and forth to town and down to Lund to see my other cousin too. It was exciting to get to take the kids to see places I knew and had seen. Grandpa Clas Magnus Sandberg had passed in 1955, so we couldn't stay with him anymore, but I took the kids to see where he and we had lived earlier. They saw my school, the church, the graveyard, and the little Thoren's store where we shopped in the village.

I took them to the Island of Visingso, where mythology has it that the big giant plopped that ground down in the middle of the Vattern Lake so his pregnant wife had a stepping stone so she could cross with ease as they were supposed to be going to visit friends. That's what the giant is supposed to be holding in his hands. (Check out the picture!) There is a big ruins on the Island where they had kept prisoners during a war, and lots of mounds that are Viking graves. There is a three hundred and fifty years old church and one that is nearly nine hundred years old. It was redone and constructed to put an observatory at the top so high school students could study the stars from it's roof.

In 1992 my step mom, Anna, and dad, Leonard thought it would be fun to go one more time to Sweden for Christmas, since it's so festive and none of us had been back for Christmas since 1946, and the three of us made plans to go. We had always revisited in the summertime.

We were supposed to spend about ten days with relatives and friends. Dad, Anna and I rented an apartment close to downtown Huskvarna and it was very spacious and plenty of comfort. We had a car to get around with so it was easy. Conrad's Photography Store was on the town square not far from where we were staying. Anna spent some of her time with an old girlfriend in another town, and then halfway through our time we went to get her to bring her to Huskvarna.

That winter they got pretty excited, as they hadn't had snow for three or four winters, but this winter they had lots of snow and they said we must have brought it with us. It would have been very disappointing if they had not had snow for Christmas while we were there, because we always remembered lots of snow in the winter there before.

We even drove down south to Lund for Christmas with the Lagnevik cousins. We stayed a couple of nights with Gullan and we got together with her son, Magnus, and family. We crammed so much visiting in with as many as we could.

Christmas Eve back up in Huskvarna, we gathered at Lars (Conrad's brother) and Ing-Britt Sandberg's for dop I grytan (dip bread in the pot of broth) and then we all went to Conrad and Maj-Britt Sandberg's house for Christmas Eve Smorgasbord dinner. What a feast she had! Their whole family was there and the house was jam packed with kids and grandchildren. Santa (Jul Tompte) came and knocked on the door and asked if there were any good girls and boys there. He doesn't come down the chimney in Sweden. Dad's old friend, Karl Frederik came to visit and have coffee with us since he knew we were leaving in a couple of days.

After dad came back from the bathroom he couldn't lift his coffee cup and was slurring his words. I was in the basement talking to Gene back home and didn't see him, until my cousin came running to get me. She felt he was having a stroke. They called an ambulance and she and her boyfriend drove Ann and me behind the ambulance to the hospital. Daddy had had not only a heart attack but a stroke as well. He and Ann had to stay an extra six weeks for him to recover at the hospital as well as some time at a nursing home. I stayed an extra ten days, but my boss at Purdue University was not very understanding and said if I didn't come home then that she didn't think she could save my job for me. I had to have that job as I had put nineteen years into my retirement and I couldn't afford to lose those years and have to start all over again at my age. My Swedish cousins could not understand this and were a bit mad at me for not staying, but they only knew how Swedes would have been treated had the situation been reversed. I think they must treat their workers better in Sweden with better understanding.

Daddy finally got to come home on February 7, 1993. We had to hire a nurse to accompany the folks and buy her a round trip ticket. I had spoken with the doctor in Sweden every day checking on his progress while they were there. He was refusing to let him go, but dad really did want to come home. He flew into Chicago and we got an ambulance to Lafayette Home Hospital and he got to see his kids and grandchildren. He was happy to see everyone, but he passed three days later on February 10, 1993. He got to be buried next to his first wife, Helen as he wished.

In 2013 I was supposed to take Kristina on a trip to Sweden as she was the only one of my children who had not been there where their roots were from. However, she felt she could not go at that time, so Jeff decided he could go with me. This turned out to be the best all around as he got sick with cancer later in 2013, and fought it for three years and passed in 2016. I am so glad we got the opportunity to go when we did, as we had a marvelous time.

We flew into Stockholm, got a car and drove up to Uppsala where Jeff wanted to do a little investigating for a book he had planned to write. There was a lot of Viking History there and that was interesting to him. Then we drove back down to Stockholm and stayed onboard the Malardrottningen ship that used to belong to Barbara Hutton. It had been a present from her father on her 21st. Birthday. It was docked in Stockholm on the Malar Lake. We got an upgrade to the Captain's quarters because Jeff knew how to negotiate. We went all over old town to see the sites. The castle was guarded by female guards now instead of male guards as in the past. We saw the people's church and City Hall where they give out the Nobel Prizes.

When we got to Granna, we stayed in a cottage at the famous resort, Gyllen Uttern. We went into the sauna several times and then into the cold showers. Very stimulating! Our view from our back deck was a beautiful sunset over the Island of Visingso. The old Kumlaby church close to 900 years old is still there full of historical stories.

Grandpa's old homestead is still there in Haurida where a young man has been renovating it and changed it from it's original yellow to the typical Swedish red and white colors. There is also still a summer house on the property and the blacksmith shop also is still there down on the corner. The new owner was very gracious and let us look around and take pictures as well.

He had chickens and cats all over the property too. There was still an outhouse and no running water inside.

We went to Thoren's country store and Inga was still there tending shop. Her brother has since passed, so she was doing it alone now.

We went to see our school houses next to the village Luthern church and the graveyard where my grandparents are buried. We brought flowers and planted and weeded the gravel plot that was squared off with granite. We visited cousins in Granna and Huskvarna as well as Jonkoping. We even went to Stalpet where my Uncle Georg had maintained the Falls for the power in the vicinity.

We had a lovely picnic with forty cousins on the Sandberg side in the Granna Park. Conrad had ordered Ostkaka (Swedish Cheesecake Pudding) that was a true delight and old time delicacy to be enjoyed by all. Jeff got to meet lots of young cousins his age, which was great.

Then Jeff and I drove down to Lund to spend a couple of days with the Lagneviks and they treated us to a lovely fish dinner. Magnus took us around campus and town to see the sites there. The next stop was at Traslovslage where Anna's daughter, Marie and Anders lived and they took us out on their big sailboat onto the ocean. It was exhilarating for sure. They have a bigger sail boat now and keep it docked in Greece. Their daughter, Jenna, is the one that I got connected with my California friends, the Mills, who took her in as a student in the Student-Abroad Program in High School.

We went over to Guthenberg (Goteborg) to see my sister Anna Lundh and her son, Roger, and three daughters, Lisa, Mimi and Nora.

It was a jam-packed trip where we made lots of memories to treasure a lifetime.

In 2020, Kristina and I were trying once again to make the trip to Sweden, but then the Covid pandemic hit us and we couldn't go. We once again had tickets for 2022, and we finally got to go and fulfilled that little dream of taking all of my children to Sweden so they could see from whence came their roots. Sadly, we only had one week to spend there, but we still got to see about thirty cousins and visit four cities. Tina truly enjoyed it, and I was proud of her for trying new foods. Ase and Jonny were very gracious hosts and Chauffeured us everywhere. Jonny and Stephen, his son, picked us up in Stockholm at the airport and drove us back to Granna where they live. They drove us to Gothenburg to see my sister Anna, her son, Roger, and daughters Mimi and Nora, then took us to Lomma near Lund to see our Lagnevik cousins. Magnus and Monica Lagnevik took us to Malmo to catch a plane back to Stockholm. We stayed the night there and flew back to Chicago via Iceland the next day. It was a quick whirlwind trip, but we packed in as much good things as we could in a short week. Now I can rest knowing that all my four kids have had the privilege of a Sweden trip.

Chapter Seven - 1975
Cottage in Haurida
Where we stayed

Chapter Seven – Trip to
Granna, Sweden - 1975
The Wooden Giant

Chapter Seven -Paris
Eiffel Tower- 1960

CHAPTER EIGHT

My First Husband-Leon(1962-1977).........

Annette-San Diego, Ca. (1963), Jeff-Chicago (1966), Mom's Passing (1969) Dad's second wedding-Anna (1970), Kristina (1971) & Jennifer (1973)-Lafayette, In.

Galations 5:20b (NIV) Acts of sinful nature are: "hatred, discord, jealousy, fits of rage, selfish ambitions."

My Poem: "The Acts of Sinful Nature"

The acts of sinful nature,
Are things that are very immature.

We don't want to practice or see,
The terrible fits of rage or selfish ambitions,
They are for the kind of people we don't want to be

Hatred, jealousy and discord,
Are never considered to be above board.

We should never wish for others'
Things, for that is jealousy
And that bothers all of us & is nothing but lousy.

Fits of rage-
Should never be written on our page,

And selfish ambitions
Should definitely be part of our contritions."

Psalm 23:4 (NIV) "Even though I walk through the valley of death, I will fear no evil, for you are with me; your rod and your staff, they comfort me."

Psalm 139 (Synopsis of the chapter) The Lord created and knows us completely and loves us thoroughly and protects us.

In a marriage you expect to have for a life time, there should be no strife with hate, rage, distrust, jealousy or selfish ambitions. We should be faithful to one another, kind, understanding and loving, but if it doesn't happen, we are delightfully pleased to find our Lord and Savior as a Comforter and a Protector.

This my Lord Jesus was for me in the midst of our divorce and his desertion of our family.

Leon wasn't always like that in the beginning. He pursued me sweetly and lovingly always saying how much he wanted a family and never liked the idea of divorce. It was furthest from either of our minds, which was why it came as a shock to all of us when he suggested it after nearly fifteen years of marriage. I had and still loved him deeply wanting to try to work things out with a counselor. He had made up his mind and didn't even want to try. He was pursuing another younger woman.

We had dated through the last two years of High School, my two years of college And his three of four years in the Navy before we got married. We never had a lot of disagreements and usually had the same family goals and aspirations. We desired to have four children, and that we were truly blessed with-even with the difficulty of receiving the last two "miracle" babies. I had miscarried three times between the second and third babies, thinking I could have no more. The doctors said I was healthy and could see no reason for my miscarriages-even the supposed experts. I miscarried my first time at the end of 1967, and I believe it was a boy, so I named him Shawn Patrick. Then in the Spring of 1968, I miscarried again and named them Michal which could be any gender. In the summer of 1969, I had my third miscarriage and named them Lauren for either gender. My names for them came later after I heard about a little boy's sister who was in heaven and she had lamented over the fact that her parents had not named her, because her mother had miscarried and did not know her gender. So I did not want my babies to feel sad because I had not named them. As I have named them, I feel I can pray for them more efficiently.

We felt with a few ups and downs if we lasted six years, we were probably meant to be together. After all, we did love each other. He was so excited as he was home on leave from the Navy in 1961. He came to visit me at my apartment in Chicago where I lived and worked at General Motors Acceptance Corporation in Accounting as an Account Clerk and Cashier.

We decided we didn't want to wait until he was discharged from the Navy to get married, so we chose the date of August 4, 1962 (while he had one year left In the Service) and just after he would be coming off a deployment to the Philippines. He would be stationed in San Diego, California, and I thought it would be fun living as a military wife in California. It was a good experience for both of us and we really had fun that year. GMAC was willing to give me a transfer to their Accounting Office in San Diego too. The PX had reasonably priced food, so we didn't have to pay a lot for groceries. We chose to live off base, so our housing cost us the most.

Our honeymoon was our trip to California. I had a little lime green station wagon I called "Sherbie" (cause it reminded me of lime sherbert.)

I gave all my cars names. My first one had been "Lady Bug" because it was an orange Volkswagen beetle bug. It got totaled by a big Buick that hit me head on while I was stopped ready to turn. This was about a year before we got married.

We loaded up my little "Sherbie" to the roof with all the stuff we thought we needed to start married life, my clothes and a few wedding presents. All we had money-wise was about $500.00 or a little less and we used that for our first apartment. The pool was just outside our double glass sliding doors and I often cooked dinner in my bathing suit and then dived in for a swim. It was the life. It took the service really long to get my spousal stipend started, and once I got to San Diego, GMAC didn't have any job waiting for me after all. For two or three weeks, Leon gave blood just so we would have food money. I got an insurance check refund from my former employer for $12.00, and the folks sent me some birthday money, so the good Lord was taking care of us until the military and GMAC came through with a job for me. We made it okay, and never took anything for granted.

We were married about four months, and I discovered I was pregnant with my first child. It would be due in about eight months-the end of August. We decided not to have the baby through the military hospital as my military girlfriend said it was a nightmare. Besides, I had good medical insurance through my job and I felt it would be better to have a regular doctor in a regular hospital. She came two weeks early and that was an experience and a half. It only cost us $25.00, so it was worth it to go that route.

I had been covering an orange crate to hold baby toiletries and diapers one morning as I worked up until two weeks before the baby was due. So I was rushing to get preparations ready. We already had the crib set up and a baby Swing.

Then something happened that I considered a nuisance. My water broke and I, being very new at this experience, didn't know how long or what to expect next as I had seen my doctor the day or two before with a stomachache, and he said, "Oh don't worry, you won't have that baby for at least two more weeks!"

So, of course, I relied on his word. I called his office and his nurse said to come on into the office so he can take another look at you. I cleaned up a bit & wore a small towel between my legs as I was dripping fairly strongly. Leon was aboard ship, so I drove myself to the doctor's office. When I got there, the office was FULL of patients, and I told the nurse I was there. After sitting there for awhile, I started to have cramps and an older lady sitting next me said," You better go tell the nurse, I think you're in labor." I said, "Oh no, all these people were ahead of me." So she went up to the desk and screamed, "That lady is in LABOR!" So I was in his office in about two minutes. The doctor, said, "Marilyn you're in labor, so go right over to the hospital." It was about 10 minutes away, but he didn't even ask me if anyone was driving me, so I drove myself over to the hospital. I had three different labor pains at the next three red lights, but I didn't worry because there was a police car at each one of those stoplights, so I felt safe. When I got to the hospital, I came in to the desk and they asked what they could do for me. I told them my name and asked if my doctor had called, and they said he had not. "Well," I said calmly, "I'm in labor." "Oh my goodness, you have to get in this wheelchair, so we can take you to delivery!" By then I was a bit frustrated and raised my voice and exclaimed, "I drove myself here, walked in on my own, and I'm not about to get in that wheelchair. I'll walk thank you!" "Oh my, you can't cause it's hospital protocol". So you know who won—they did, of course! I had gotten there about 12:30 PM, and she was born about 3:03PM. Most women would be thrilled to only have about a two and a half hour labor time. That's pretty quick for the first one and especially two weeks earlier than the original delivery date estimated. They just barely had time to prep me. When I first got there, I called Leon aboard ship and told him where I was, and he was so surprised, he said, "Why?" I asked him if he had forgotten we were having a baby. He asked how I had gotten there, and when I told him I drove, he said, "How am I supposed to get there?" I told him to take a cab and stop by the house to get my packed suitcase to bring along for me. When I left for the doctor's office that morning, I had no idea I'd be needing my hospital suitcase at that time.

My folks had planned to be there when I went to the hospital, but since she came early, they didn't get there until a week after she was born. When they got there, I met them at the door and had a hot meal ready for them. They were pretty surprised as they had planned to come help Leon was very thrilled that we got a girl first, as that is what he wanted, and he wanted to name her "Annette" after the Mickey Mouse Club star, Annette Funicello. I thought "Yvonne" fit nicely for a second name after one of my favorite cousins in Kansas City. After a few days, the folks decided to drive back home to Lafayette, Indiana bringing Annette and me for a visit, and Leon would follow in about two weeks or so to pick us up to bring us back to California. The big surprise to me when he got there was that he said, "We're staying now that I'm out of the service. I sold all our furniture, and the Navy packed up all our personal stuff and is shipping it to Lafayette." I was shocked as he had not discussed this with me at all and just decided on his own to do this.

We had talked about staying in California after he was discharged from the Navy, so it was not only a shock to me, but a disappointment as well. I liked it there.

I guess things happen for reasons sometimes unknown, because now I'm glad we settled in the Midwest. While Leon and I did not find work in Lafayette, we ended up moving to Chicago where I got my job back at GMAC. Leon decided to try to go to Wright Junior College for an education. He stayed home during the day with the baby while I worked and he attended classes in the evening. As normal, he decided school was not for him. He drove a taxi part of the time and then got a driver's job driving for Shulton cosmetic company. Since I had a savings plan through GMAC, I had $2,000.00 saved up so we decided to buy a three-apartment building. We rented out the first and third floor apartments and lived in the largest one on the second floor on Grace Street near six corners. There was a handy little family-owned neighborhood grocery store on one corner and a grade school just two blocks in the other direction where Annette went to kindergarten and first grade.

In 1965, I got pregnant with a second child, and it ended up being a boy. We didn't have all that fancy equipment like they do today, so our births' genders were surprises until the day they were born. I know sometimes today young people like to be surprised and don't ask for gender detection prior to birth, but I think it's rare. Of course if one knows ahead of time, they can have the proper clothes planned ahead. I bought a lot of yellow, mint green, and acqua sleepers and blankets.

Since Leon had an Irish heritage, I thought the name "Shawn Patrick" would be good for our little boy, but Leon would not hear of it. My dad's middle name was Patrick too, so I really liked the idea of it. We both finally agreed on "Jeffrey Scott" for his name and he, like his sister, came two weeks early on February 13,1966- one day before Valentine's Day. The doctor in Chicago, who delivered him was named Valentine too. So he asked me If I was going to name him "Valentine" and I said, "No, don't believe I will!" without even asking Leon. He was born on a Sunday at our denominational "Swedish Covenant Hospital" on Foster Avenue. In Chicago, Illinois.

Chicago became special to Jeff over the years as he ended up going to college there at my alma mater, North Park College, and living and working there for a time. He also met his wife Joanna there as well. Coincidentally, she had gone to Purdue University which was in my and our later home town of Lafayette, In. We continued to live in Chicago until 1970 until Jeff was almost four. My mother passed away in 1969 at the age of sixty-three. The folks had been visiting us in Chicago in June of 1969 and she and I were attending a denominational annual Conference at North Park College for a couple of days. Mother had not felt real well prior to this, but she wanted to go. Her pastor brother, Rev. Kenneth Swanson, and his wife were attending the same conference from Duluth, Minnesota and were staying in one of the dorm rooms on campus. The last day of the Conference, June 18, 1969, she felt like she wanted to rest in between meetings, so went to lie down in their room. The last meeting together was a big Communion Service in the chapel, and Mother wanted to attend, so she came down to meet and sit with me. It was quite lovely and very meaningful. After it was over, we went back to our apartment and I fixed supper for all of us before the folks took off for home in Lafayette. It was about a three-hour drive, so they were anxious to get on the road. I didn't know until later that Mother had been rather sick the night before and had sat up in the big overstuffed chair most of the night. Had I known that, I would have insisted we take her to the hospital, which she would have probably refused to do. We were planning to go to Lafayette for a visit the next weekend, and she said before they left that she would have a roast, potatoes and carrots ready for us when we got there. I told her not to worry about that, we could pick something up on the way. Swedes always worry about having food ready for their guests, and mother always fussed to be a good hostess.

Mother never made the roast, but it wasn't because she didn't want to. Mother never made it home.

About one half hour after they left, Dad called me and said, "I think Mother is gone." I collapsed onto the floor sobbing and Leon took the phone. He found out they were at a hospital in the southern part of Chicago, so Leon said we'd be right there as soon as we could. We left the kids with our neighbor friends, the Casellis and were on our way. I can't remember at what point we called my brother. When we got to the hospital, Mother was lifeless, but still warm, and I wailed, "Can't you do anything for her?" They said that there was no use as she was gone when Dad brought her in. They had stopped at a filling station bathroom earlier when she complained of a stomachache, but when she finally came out, she collapsed by the car. The service station attendant assisted Dad in getting her into the back seat and he told him where the nearest hospital was.

We went back home to pack and get the children and followed dad back to Lafayette. The ambulance brought mother to Soller-Baker Funeral Home in Lafayette after the coroner examined her in Chicago.

Ralph and Kathy came shortly after and the next three days before the funeral were very difficult. Kathy and I did not feel like eating and we felt empty in Mother's kitchen not having her there with us. Leon's mother said she would keep our kids while we went to mother's funeral, and I thought maybe that was best as I knew dad would probably need me to help keep him bolstered up. Later I had wished they were there with us, because that was their grandma.

It probably was the best in the long run though.

Dad was so lonely, so we stayed a while until Kathy and I found a housekeeper for dad, as he did not want to be alone in that house with mother gone. We actually found someone that dad thoroughly approved of and that he knew. His cousin's ex-wife, Jean, lived in town and was agreeable to come live in the house and cook and clean for him. So this worked out for about a year.

Later, dad found out his old Swedish friend, Anna Walgren's husband had passed away about the same time that Mother had. They started corresponding and talking on the phone on a regular basis, and then Dad thought he'd go visit her in Jamestown, New York. However, he thought it best if he took one of his granddaughters with him. Annette was seven at the time, and she was excited to get to go with grandpa to New York.

Anna was very impressed how organized Annette was at seven and how she laid out her hair ribbons and matching socks for each dress every morning.

Dad & Anna were getting re-acquainted pretty quickly from when they had known each other in Rockford, Illinois, so dad decided to bring her back to Lafayette to see how she might like it. She stayed a short time and they decided to get married.

There was not much time to plan anything and they didn't want any of us at their ceremony. They chose an old friend (a couple from Wales), The Thomases, to stand up as witnesses for them, and I had a small get together with a cake for them afterwards.

Ralph was a bit upset that he wasn't included, but I told him it happened so fast that I didn't even have time to plan much and I wasn't even invited to the ceremony. They ended up actually getting married on my birthday-August 29, 1970.

Dad and Anna went back to New York to sell Anna's house and I think it was a good idea, because dad was such a good businessman, and Anna said she didn't think she could have gotten that good of a deal.

Ann brought back some of her treasures and pictures that meant a lot to her, so she could make things more like her own.

The house had been built only about eight years before, so things were still fairly new.

Ann had a bit of a different personality than my mom's, but she was good for dad anyway. He still missed my mom, but he discovered one could love more than one woman no matter how different they were. Dad always felt pretty fortunate that God allowed him to be blessed by two good Swedish wives.

They were married about twenty-two years. Ann stayed in the house for about eight months before deciding to move back to Jamestown to be close to her daughter, Doris Bergfeldt and her first husband Charles's grave after Dad passed away. She had two granddaughters, Wendy and Laurie that were both married by then. They became part of our extended family as well. We didn't get to see them a lot as they lived so far away, but we always had fun with them when we could get together.

Dad always loved being around people and often asked Ann if they could have folks over for coffee or a meal. Ann loved that too and was always pretty gracious about all the company. They had friends and relatives visiting from Sweden occasionally as well. We would take turns for the holidays and I would have Thanksgiving at my house and Ann would have us all there at their house on Christmas Eve, as that was when we Swedes would celebrate Christmas. We would have evening dinner with all the Swedish customary dishes, open presents, and then go to church for the Christmas Eve candlelight service about nine o'clock. The children would always be so excited after supper to start opening their packages. We would kind of draw it out and tell them we had to wash dishes first, and they would get so antsy.

Ann always made all the traditional Swedish Smorgasbord dishes that most of us loved. My kids never did get the affection for pickled herring (sill) like the folks and I did though. I made peppar kakor (gingerbread cookies), drommar (dream cookies), spritz cookies, and my Swedish coffee bread that I made every Christmas. Ann had her sister's homemade cheese she sent from Sweden, and Ann's homemade potato sausage. We used to be able to buy good Swedish rye bread (Limpa) from a Swedish deli on Clark Street in Chicago. There was, of course, our pickled herring, pickled beets, and sliced cumbers in salt & vinegar water, deviled eggs, sylta (head cheese)-usually homemade, ham, rice pudding, meat balls and lingon berries, brown sweet beans cooked with a cinnamon stick and knacke brod (dry flat bread)-similar to rye crisp which Jeff just loved.

To top it all off we had warm fruit soup (frukt soppa) with lots of whipped cream. It was a feast to behold and also to eat. I have tried through the years to continue all of these traditions, but I'm not sure the kids really appreciate all of these foods, let alone even like them.

They may miss them some day after I'm gone, but I have taught some of the girls and granddaughters how to bake my bread and I left them all the recipes if they ever get in the mood to make them. Anna taught my middle daughter, Kristina, how to make kaldarmar (cabbage rolls), but I think she has perfected them even more, as she makes them so delicious.

One special Swedish cake (like a spongy pound cake) is called a torte that was Grandma Ann's recipe, is smothered in whipped cream as a coating is one of Jen's favorites and I try sometimes to make it for her birthday as often as I can. I just made it this year on 9-11-22 for her birthday.

These Swedish traditions were very much a part of our family all the way from our first daughter, Annette being born in San Diego, California in 1963, through Jeffrey Scott coming in Chicago, Illinois, in 1966. Even though I lost three babies after Jeff, we continued the traditions into 1971 in Lafayette, Indiana, where Kristina was born and Jennifer followed in Lafayette in 1973.

Dad's second wife, Anna, who was also Swedish, helped us carry on all these Swedish traditions on as well after they married in 1970.

Chapter Eight – My First Car
"Lady Bug" - 1960

Chapter Eight – My
Second Car "Sherbie"
1962

Chapter Eight 8-4-1962
Leon & Marilyn
Fleeger's Wedding

Chapter Eight – Dad & Ann

Chapter Eight ~~The~~ Fleeger Family-1972 Annette-9, Jeff-6, & Kristina-1

~~Chapter Eight – The~~
Fleeger Family-1975
Annette-12, Jeff-9,
Tina-4, & Jen-2

Chapter Eight – My Kids 2010
Annette, Jeff, Tina, & Jen

CHAPTER NINE

Flying Experiences (1975-1977)

Leon had always wanted to learn to fly a small plane, so after he looked into that possibility at Purdue University Airport, he decided to go ahead and sign up for lessons. After he discovered how much renting a plane and paying for an instructor would cost, he decided to check out the possibility of buying a plane and keeping it at the airport and renting it out to students who needed a plane for lessons. When we discovered he could make the payments on the plane by renting it out, he felt that was the best way to go, and then we would just have to pay for the instructor.

He decided to buy it new and it was a four-seater Cessna. It was light blue and white and had the number of N4347R on it's tail. He encouraged me to take flying lessons as well. We got the same male instructor, named Larry. Lee had gone ahead of me and started his lessons first. I'll never forget my first lesson-it will be burned into my memory forever. I don't know if Larry did this to all his new students or not, but after he had shown me a few maneuvers, he asked if I wanted to have some fun. I said, "Ok!" never dreaming what would follow. He started making lazy circles in the sky and then almost immediately started spiraling toward the ground like he was going to take a nose dive straight into the earth. I took a deep breath, said absolutely nothing, and waited for the spinning to stop. He said, "Did that scare you?" I said, "Well, I wasn't sure what the purpose of that little stunt was for, but I figured you'd explain it to me." He said he wanted to show me what could sometimes happen and how you can pull yourself out of it. I told him I wasn't sure what I should do in that kind of situation, but you surely gave my tummy the flip flops. He said he was impressed with my composure. We took lessons for a short time from Larry and then switched over to a female instructor named Ann. She was quite proficient, and smart women always intrigued Leon. She also was practicing to be a stunt flyer and came from up near Joliet. She taught however at the Purdue airport as well as Larry had. She eventually became a pilot for Delta Air Lines south of here. Leon started taking more and more flight lessons and was gone from home much too often. He took his cross-country lesons to Florida with her as his Instructor. So as not to make it look suspicious, they took Ann's younger brother and our Annette along. I was none the wiser as I trusted him. Leon sold our camper to pay for my lessons so I could get my pilot's license; however, I never got that money nor the rest of my lessons, as he used it to buy new clothes so he'd look good to the younger woman—Ann. One evening when I had dinner ready and Grandma Brady was staying with us, Leon appeared in a new outfit and announced he was going for an unscheduled flying lesson and also added that he wasn't hungry. As soon as he left, Grandma Brady opened my eyes. She expressed concern that I should wake up and smell the coffee. Pretty smart of an eighty-some to notice while I didn't. Sometimes when conspicuous bad things are going on we may be the last to see them, because we don't want them to be true.

I expressed to Lee that I wanted to go talk to Ann after he expressed to me his interest in her. He forbid me to do that. Since she moved away I figured she might be trying as hard to get away from him as I was trying to keep him. Since I never saw her again, I never knew for sure.

In 1975, when I took Annette and Jeff on our trip to Sweden, Leon had driven his motorcycle South to visit Ann and had a bad accident on a curve. He got pretty banged up, but he did not want his brother or my sister-in-law to let me know. He said he didn't want to ruin my trip and for me to feel like I had to come home. Truth be told, he probably didn't want me to find out where he was going. Later he took the little girls on a camping trip with Ann and he told Tina not to say anything to Grandma and Grandpa when they got home and, of course, the first thing a kid will do is tell something to someone they were told not to.

I was pretty alert to things after Grandma put me on the alert to watch for things.

Once soon after, he said he was going to Indianapolis to learn how to fly a mail route, so would I take him to the bus station to catch a bus to Indianapolis so he could go down there to do that. I did, and I asked him if he wanted me to wait until his bus came. No, he said I didn't need to do that. He said it would be there shortly. I got to thinking and called the bus station when I got home and asked if the bus for Indianapolis was on time and if it had left yet. They said there were no buses today for Indianapolis-in fact, there wouldn't be any until the next morning. I also knew that if anyone was going to take a plane out, they had to file a flight plan, so I went to the Purdue Airport to check to see if a flight plan had been filed for our plane. Sure enough, there WAS a flight plan to go South and it was filed by none other than Mr. Leon Fleeger! I knew he had to be back before Monday so he could go to work, so I was waiting at the airport Sunday evening at seven PM. The surprised look on his face could not hide his shame and confusion. He was CAUGHT! He said, "How did you know?" I told him to count it up to feminine suspicion. He didn't deny he had been to see Ann.

Leon really did turn out to be a very good pilot and I'll never forget our first out of town flight to Chicago to the tiny little landing strip by Lake Michigan with three sides of the strip were encircled by water. It was quite scary, especially when we came back to take off and go home. The strip was pretty short and you had to be precise and good to maneuver it.

We knew they closed that airport at midnight and we had had an evening in town with my brother and sister-in-law, and were hurrying to get back with only ten minutes to spare. After we got the engine warmed up and ready to take off, they turned the runway lights off. They knew we were ready to go, so I felt that was really irresponsible of them to turn them off before we got off the runway. We couldn't see anything as it was so dark, but thankfully Leon was able to maneuver us into a flight path without overrunning the runway. You have to be able to land a plane alone before you can get your pilot license, so I never got that far with my lessons. However, I did know how to fly the plane. Leon let me fly a lot, but then I would always let him land when we got to our destination.

One January we flew to Kansas City to visit my cousin, Vonnie, and Lee was so tired that he told me to fly home so he could sleep, which he did. It was so cold we had to pull the plane into the hanger before taking off to deice the wings. I did just fine and woke Lee up when we got to Purdue to land the plane. I was pretty proud of myself for getting us home without getting lost or needing any help from Lee until we got to the airport. The folks had been staying with the kids at our house and our furnace had gone out and it was fifteen degrees below zero. They were all bundled together in one bed to stay warm. I said, "My goodness, why didn't you go down to your house to get warm?" They didn't think of it they said. So guess it was cold everywhere.

When my Dad got colon cancer and went to the Mayo Clinic in Rochester, Minnesota for surgery, we went up to Chicago to pick Ralph and Kathy up to go with us in the plane to go see the folks in Minnesota. Dad was really surprised we came. It's times like this that made having a plane wonderful. I think Ralph was impressed with Leon and his abilities.

Leon kept going out flying all he could, but I never was able to get my license. One had to fly solo and land solo in order to get their license. I had only done that with an instructor, so I didn't have enough flying hours to complete that feat. Leon even took glider lessons, and that scared me as they didn't even have an engine, and they had to rely on the wind to carry them wherever they flew. Leon was very good at maneuvering machinery though, so did a fine job. That's probably why he was so good at handling the big fire trucks he drove on the Lafayette Fire Department. He also drove school buses and athletic buses for Purdue University on his off days.

Leon always had an affinity for smart women, so I guess I shouldn't be surprised that he had an interest in our instructor, When he said he was interested in her, I expressed an interest that I wanted to talk to her, and he forbid me to do that. Since she moved away I figured she might be trying as hard to get away from him as I was trying to keep him. Since I never saw her again, I never knew for sure.

Leon started taking more and more flight lessons and was gone from home much too often. He took his cross-country lessons to Florida with Ann as his instructor. So as not to make it look suspicious, they took Annette, our daughter, and Ann's little brother along. I was none the wiser as I trusted him.

Leon sold our camper to pay for the rest of my lessons so I could get my license, but I never got that money nor the rest of my lessons, as he used it to buy new clothes so he'd look good to the younger woman-Ann. one evening when I had dinner ready to put on the table for the family, and Grandma Brady was staying with us, Leon appeared in a new flashy outfit and announced that he was not hungry and was going for an unscheduled flight lesson. As soon as he left, Grandma Brady opened my eyes. She expressed concern that I should wake up and smell the coffee. Pretty smart of an eighty-something lady to notice while I didn't. Sometimes when conspicuous bad things are going on we may be the last to see them, because we don't want them to be true.

In 1975, when I took Annette and Jeff to Sweden for a visit, Leon had driven his motorcycle South to visit Ann and had a bad accident on a curve. He got pretty banged up, but he did not want his brother or sister-in-law to let me know. He said he didn't want to ruin our trip so I'd feel like I had to come home. Truth be told, he probably didn't want me to know where he was going. Later, he took the two little girls on a camping trip with Ann and told Tina not to tell Grandma and Grandpa who they went with. Of course, the first thing a kid will do, is tell something to someone they were told not to.

Once soon after, he said he was going to Indianapolis to learn how to fly a mail route, so would I take him to the bus station to catch a bus to Indianapolis so he could go down there to do that. He said it would be there shortly, and that I didn't need to wait with him. I got to thinking and called the bus station when I got home and asked if the bus for Indianapolis was on time and if it had left yet. They said there were no buses to Indianapolis today-in fact, there wouldn't be any until tomorrow morning. I also knew that if anyone was going to take a plane out, they had to file a flight plan, so I went to Purdue Airport where our plane was kept, and sure enough, a flight plan had been filed for our plane to go South, and it had been filed by none other than by Mr. Leon Fleeger! I knew he had to be back before Monday so he could go to work, so I was waiting at the airport Sunday evening at seven PM. The surprised look on his face could not hide his shame and confusion. He was CAUGHT! He said, "How did you know?" I told him to count it up to feminine intuition and suspicion. He did not deny he had been to see Ann.

The last we ever heard of our instructor was that while she was practicing her stunt flying maneuvers near Joliet, her home stomping grounds, she had a fatal accident and ran her plane nose first into the ground. Sometimes when you're flipping you can get pretty disoriented. I always felt bad about that. She really was a good pilot.

Leon and I ended up divorced anyway.

Thank the Lord, my children all grew up to be well-adjusted successful adults with fruitful lives. I am so proud of all of them and their wonderful spouses and children. I am a blessed happy grandma and great grandmother as well.

~~Chapter Nine~~ Our Cessna
Four-seater Plane 1976
4347 Romeo

CHAPTER TEN

My Second Husband-Vernon (1979-1981).. Country Living

Besides feeling disappointed, hurt, and rejected, I was somewhat lonely after Leon left us. I dated a few different fellows. A policeman, a school teacher, a co-worker, a painter, but none of them intrigued me. Finally my sister-in-law, Ruth, introduced me to a guy named Vernon. He was okay, while he was trying to impress me, but we dated for a while and he was good to my dad, and did things for him, so he won him over before me. When someone is trying to make a good impression, they do and say all the nice things. I still wasn't sure he was right for me--for us. If I was going to get married again, I wanted it to be right for the children as well. When he asked me to marry him, I refused him not feeling like it was perfect. He kept begging me to marry him, saying he had lost his four children, and he said he could help me raise my four children. His parents were strong Jehovah Witnesses, but he was not a practicing one. In fact, he started to come to church with me to show me how dedicated he was trying to be to me and my church.

He bought an old farm house, and had it moved to a lot he bought out on 200 South, which is also called Hagerty Lane, closer to town. He said what a wonderful place to raise children. He was handy at many things, and he said he could teach Jeff, my son, a lot. I knew he needed attention and guidance from an adult male, because now at the age of eleven, he was really missing out. Vern kept begging and begging me to get married, so I broke down and asked the children what they thought of the idea. They all seemed to be in favor of it and said, "Whatever makes you happy, Mom."

So we planned a summer wedding in a beautiful spot at the Purdue Horticulture Park out on 26 in West Lafayette, Indiana. It was a beautiful spot and we chose a spot under a big sprawling tree.

He knew how much I loved lavender, so he bought me a lavender dress and brought it to my house to give me to wear during the wedding. A little unusual, but I did like it. It fit and was very simple, so that's what I wore.

We did not have a regular minister at the time, so I asked another local minister to officiate our wedding. He had been my Christian Counselor I had confided in when Leon and I had been going through our divorce. Leon had refused to go, but I felt I needed some guidance.

Living in the country had some benefits, with good schools, a nice family next door with children. We had a big garden and the children pretty much were confined to home and couldn't be wondering off to the neighbors like they did in town. They had chores and helped me in the garden weeding and picking vegetables. Our big Collie dog loved the big yard, and Vern taught him how to stay out of the busy road and within the perimeter of the property. He built him a big dog house so he could get out of any bad weather.

At first things went okay, but Vern gradually started being verbally abusive to me and the children. They were not allowed to speak at the table or in the living room when he was watching his ball games. They weren't allowed to ever watch anything on television that they wanted. Vern always had a ball game on. His discipline was always stern and never with love.

His attention toward my fifteen-year-old daughter began to be questionable. He kept playboy magazines in boxes in the basement, and I didn't care for the fact that Jeff ran across them.

When I asked if he would get rid of them or find a better hiding place, he refused.

One night after I had gone to bed early, Annette had come downstairs for a snack as she often did. Vern got a picture of a nude fat lady and plastered Annette's face on it and put it on the refrigerator, and said to Annette, "If you don't quit eating so much, you're going to look like this." Not only was it hurtful, but exceedingly distasteful and very disturbing to her.

I was awakened out of a sound sleep hearing a scuffle on the side porch. Annette had called her then boyfriend, Darin, crying telling him of the incident, and he came out to the country on his motorcycle to confront Vern and was determined to take Annette to his house where his parents were to get her away from Vern. I got up to witnessing Vern and Darin tumbling off the porch into the yard. Darin drove off with Annette without saying anything to me. After that Annette went to live with her dad. We had quite a few words over this incident.

Leon had an apartment building where they first lived, but he eventually got married to a gal that wasn't always nice to Annette. When Vern got nasty with Jeff, he also went to live with them. She had two boys that were always trying to get Jeff in trouble, and even lied about things. One day when their mother repeated this lie to Leon, he didn't even ask Jeff his version of the story, and started pounding on him. This just compounded more hurt on Jeff that he had earlier received from his dad and also Vern. When I found all of everything out later, I had had my fill of both Lee and Vern, and decided to leave and try to find a house to rent and take my children away from all the turmoil. Although I had kept my house, I had it rented out with a lease, and couldn't get it back yet for a few months until Spring, and it was still winter.

Leon had bought the old homeplace on Center from me when I bought our house on Catula and usually rented it out. However Center was empty at this time, and it's always hard to rent out a house in the winter. Leon and I did try to help each other out from time to time when we needed it, so I asked him if I could rent it for a few months until we could get my Catula house back. I told him I couldn't pay the amount of rent he had been getting, but that I could pay what his mortgage payment was. After all, it was better than letting it sit empty in the winter. Besides, I said, this is for your children. so he agreed to that. After that we were able to go back to our home on Catula.

The day I decided to leave Vern, there was about two feet of snow in a very long driveway. As soon as Vern went to work at Purdue, I shoveled that long driveway out and started packing boxes and went and got a moving uhaul truck and carried all the boxes out to it. Since I couldn't carry out the heavy furniture I had there, I told Vern when he got home that I was leaving and he could help get the heavy stuff out. He was very surprised, but didn't try to talk me out of it then. I am a very determined person and once I make up my mind to something, I usually follow through. Even though I moved out, he tried for a while to talk me into coming back. I told him I had had my fill and I would never put up with his shenanigans again.

I told him he was verbally abusive to both the kids and me, and I would never put up with that again. His extreme depravity was probably the cruelest of his abuses.

I did not file for divorce immediately, but since it was nearly two years of this nonsense, I finally decided to file. I didn't see much of him after that. I asked nothing of him except to leave us alone. Our divorce was finalized in 1981.

Chapter Ten Second Husband ~~Vern~~ 1979-1980

CHAPTER ELEVEN

My Working Years – 1975-2003

Tippecanoe County Sheriff's Department...1975-1989
Purdue University.1989-2003
MY Alone Years 1981-1989

While Leon and I were married, I worked at Purdue Accounting Dept. when we first came from Chicago, until I quit to have Kristina, our third child in 1971. In 1977, for a few months after our divorce, I worked at Howard Johnson's restaurant as a waitress to sustain my income to feed and house my children with only a small stipend from my ex-husband. I continued it for another six months or so after I was hired on at the Sheriff's Department. After those two jobs were a bit too much for me to continue, I dropped the waitressing job. After a while, I realized $9,200. a year was not enough to raise four kids on and to make a house payment, and buy food and clothes. I made some, but now didn't have much time to do that anymore either.

I worked at first in the Court House, then in the front office on 6th street. I left the department just as they were building the new jail on Duncan Road. I would answer calls, take care of walk-ins, take finger prints for gun permits, take care of reference checks, expunge old records that were requested by other Police Departments or attorneys. I also kept the meal records, but my main job was to receive all the court papers to be served such as bench warrants, writs of attachments, evictions, notices, etc. to be served by my five process servers.

Then I was to type service returns on the back and return them to the perspective courts. They were a great bunch of guys. I worked for three different Sheriffs. John Rusk hired me, then I worked for Edgar Harger who had come from the State Police Department and then finally for David Heath over fourteen and a half years.

From there, I went to Purdue University to work again in the Accounting Department. I hired in as a Supervisor to the Data Entry Department and then did data entry as an Account Clerk from 1989-2003 until I retired. This was a must as Gene's Altzheimer's was getting worse and he really needed me at home to take care of him.

Since I had previously worked for Purdue's Accounting Department in 1970-1971 for about a year and a half before I had Kristina, I was able to add that year and half to my fourteen and half years for my retirement service period. In fact, another reason I wanted to go to Purdue and work again was because they had the same retirement program that the Sheriff's Department had, and so I had tucked away thirty years in retirement, and they gave me an extra year for each five years I had worked if I would retire by December of 2003, which gave me a total of thirty-three years for my retirement pay. That was equivalent to my social security, so I was pleased with that. If anything happened to me, the same amount was to go to Gene, as he was no longer working.

I truly feel sorry for young folks now days because most companies do not have retirement programs for them to get any retirement pays. In fact, the companies want to kick them out if they get a little past fifty.

Young folks today have to learn how to plan ahead and put their own plans into play and save for their own retirements. I don't think a lot of companies even have 401 K plans they pay into either. It's pretty much left up to the individual to plan well ahead if they want to retire some day. I guess I was born at the right time in history to have what I have. I still don't think I'm paid what I should have in my social security, but the government is even threatening to dispense with that all together in due time. I guess the government may want the public to depend on everyone being at their mercy and turn it all into Socialism. Yuk! I can't think of anything worse! I hope our young people don't ever let that come to pass.

Chapter Eleven Fleeger Home
~~1976~~ –2006 – 1513 Catula Ave.

Chapter Eleven Fleeger Kids
1981 ~~Annette~~–18, Jeff-15,
Tina-10, & Jen-8

Chapter Eleven ~~Fleeger Kids – 1985~~
Annette-22, Jeff-19, Tina-14,& Jen-12

~~Chapter Eleven 1976~~ – Sheriff
John Rusk-Tippecanoe Co.

Chapter Eleven 1985
Sheriff Edgar Harger
Tippecanoe County

Chapter Eleven- Fleeger Kids 1987
Jeff-21, Tina-16, Jen-14

CHAPTER TWELVE

Our Swedish Traditions And Holidays

From May to December, Swedes like to get away to the mountains for a little retreat. In March, there is a historic ski race in Mora, which is a small town in Dalarna Province called the VASA RACE. It's a forty-eight mile marathon with 1100 hardy cross-country skiers taking part to replicate Gustaf Vasa fleeing his enemies, the Danes, in 1521. He chased out the Danes and put an end to to the foreign occupation of his country. This course is so difficult that usually only 100 today reach the finish line. Since in winter time, days grow dark at 2:00 PM, folks anxiously await the warmth of the Spring sun and beautiful wild flowers of the forest.

Anxious for the colorful look of Spring, folks purchase sprigs of silver birch and tie gaily colored chicken feathers to them to celebrate Easter.

When March 21st arrives, it is the spring equinox, which means Spring is officially here. This means crisp biscuit-thin Swedish waffles with jam and whipped cream will be served. The children love to welcome Spring this way.

The Swedish nation are tremendous sun-worshippers and as soon as they see any amount of sun rays, they are out soaking it up after a long winter's time. folks love a stroll in the woods and coming upon a fragile snowdrop flower, a yellow crocus or a wood anemone or the white or blue sippa wild flower is very much a treat. Later in the summer will be an abundance of priests collars (daisies), and marguerites. In fact, my little kitty I had in Sweden in 1946, I had named "Sippa" after the wild flower.

At Easter time, they celebrate with little Easter witches on a broomstick with a copper kettle and black cat the Saturday before Easter. They wear a shawl, kerchief, and apron. Little children dress up this way and ring a doorbell, shaking their kettles looking for sweets much as children do during Halloween. They enjoy decorating eggs as well and serving them on Saturday before Easter.

When the last day of April comes, the student who has passed the stiff matriculation exam is entitled to wear the distinctive "students cap", a peaked white velvet cap. It's a source of pride. Then comes the oral exam. They are wooed in song in five University towns, and particularly in the two oldest. Upsalla and Lund. Students fling their caps into the air. This is called "Hightimeliness" (Hogtidlighet) before a speaker speaks. Old and new students alike celebrate the threshold of summer. "Long may it live!" A big bonfire is started on a hill to frighten away witches and trolls. This is called "Walpurgis Eve".

May 1 is a public holiday. Numerous workers' organizations form a parade through the streets. It can be a reminder to the older generation of the new ideas they once fought so hard and successfully for. It's no longer a revolt, but an accepted annual eremony. It was a battle for Socialism and now the working class own cars, boats, flats, summer cottages, etc. Little children enjoy hanging mayday baskets on door knobs filled with wild flowers.

June 6 is Swedish Flag Day. A golden sun in a clear blue sky (Stockholm, the capital, has a ceremony.)

It's a day I fly my Swedish Flag too! With pride! Blue and yellow is everywhere with the blue lakes, yellow cornfields and wheatfields against the blue sky with blue eyes and blond-haired girls. Sweden claims their flag to be the oldest national standard of Europe. This very flag of a yellow cross on a blue background was the flag adopted by Constantine the Great. It's a token of 150 consecutive years of peaceful relations with the rest of the world.

Midsummer is the third Saturday of June (the first day of Summer). The celebration comes the day before where a midsummer pole is erected in the shape of a cross and decorated with two wreaths of flowers and folks sing and dance in costume around the pole. A little ditty they sing, goes like this:

Sma graderna, sma graderna, ar lystiga att se. Ej oron, ej oron, ej svansa har va de. Oh jak, jak, jak, o jak, jak, jak, jak, jak, etc. Adults as well as children look silly, but have fun dancing around the pole and singing this funny little song. When we were there in 1975, my two oldest kids loved participating in this ritual and wanted a pole the next summer at home in the States during Midsummer. Such crazy fun!

This is also a time when men ready their boats with new varnish. The Swedish Vikings started their long journeys that took them as far as Russia for their raids.

In July most Swedes can take a three-four week holiday or vacation.

The midnight sun is a sight to see. It is such a joy in June and July to be able To even read a newspaper outside at midnight in this land of the midnight sun. Of course, in the wintertime the downside is that it gets dark at about 2:00- 2:30 in the afternoon.

Everywhere couples dance to Swedish music of fast waltzes, schottisches, polkas, and the intricate hambo which Daddy and Ann loved to dance to and it was a joy to watch them. After all, dance halls were where young people, back in the earlier days, used to go meet each other and have fun. In fact, there's a funny story daddy tells about in Rockford, Illinois, where he and Ann met when they were young. He went into the dance hall and wanted to talk to Ann, and she didn't want to leave, so he picked her up and slung her over his shoulder and carried her out. So much for that! Guess she talked and listened then. Crazy young people!

Summer is the time for Swedes to return to nature. A time to exodus to their summer cottages in the woods or by the sea or a lake. In the summer, three fourths of the town is on holiday. Since WWII, many travel abroad to explore other cultures. And wouldn't you know it, many go to tropical places where there are beaches and plenty of sun, especially during the colder months.

August 8 is crayfish time. Such a delicacy! Hjortron (cloud berry), a small yellow berry, that resembles a small raspberry, grows in Northern swamplands. It tastes a little like burnt carmel. It's a little rare and expensive. They make it into jams and even the drink snaps.

Many parents take night classes to help further their children's education at home.

In August and September, there are many mushrooms and berries in the woods for Swedes to pick and enjoy. Especially the red whortleberry (called lingon). It's a wild Swedish cranberry-type which is sweeter and smaller than our cranberries.

It is very high in antioxidants and very healthy for us. Dr. Oz recently reported on the benefits of this fruit. Swedes enjoy their juice and preserve-like sauce we all enjoy with rice pudding, meatballs or any meat. I couldn't keep enough lingon on hand when my non-Swedish French husband discovered how good it was on everything. Yum! They have plenty of bilberry and blueberries. Their wild raspberries are sweeter than the garden variety. Wild Rose Hips (Nippon) soup is a dessert and is good with whipped cream as all of these fruits are when they are cooked into a crème. Swedish mushrooms (svamp) are also plentiful. One must be careful there as here to avoid the poisonous ones.

The Swedes do their census every October, which is public to everyone. One can't hide their age or income.

Darkness plagues Swedish homes in the winter except for the interior lighting.

On the first Sunday of Advent, all Swedes use a four-candlestick brass holder to put in their windows. They light the first one and let it burn shortly. They use all white candles. On the second Sunday of Advent, they light the first two candles for a while and soon until the fourth Sunday, the candles look like a small row of organ pipes. It means that Christmas is almost here. This is either placed on their windowsill or the middle of the table for all to see. A star of Bethlehem is placed in their window when Advent begins. This dark month of December in this Northern land is brightened with lots of candles.

NOBEL DAY – December 1O

On Nobel Day, the flag is raised. The Swedish Academy in Stockholm, the capital, presents for the Literature Prize with a diploma from the King is presented. There are also prizes for Physics, Chemistry, Medicine and Physiology. The ceremony lasts for two hours with speeches. The Peace Prize is awarded in Oslo, Norway by the Norwegian Parliament. There is an enormous banquet at the Town Hall following the ceremonies.

The year that Professor Brown from Purdue University received his Chemistry Prize, I kept a scrapbook for him of all the Journal and Courier daily newspaper articles of the awards. I presented it to him upon his return from Sweden and he was thrilled. In fact when he retired and was cleaning out his office, he ran across the scrapbook he had forgotten about, and now was rehashing and enjoying those joyous times. He called to thank me again for that gesture. I especially enjoyed reading about his reactions to Sankta Lucia Day on December 13th in Stockholm. It was early on December 13, before sunup and there was a knock on his door. A lady dressed in a long white gown, with a crown of lit candles on her head, St. Lucia, was bringing him coffee and Lucia saffron rolls bright and early, which is a Swedish custom and tradition. He was half asleep and not familiar with this tradition and he thought he was dreaming and that an angel was at the door. I have some funny stories of when I portrayed St. Lucia at the jail as well.

Sankta Lucia Day is a story of a Sicilian girl from about 800AD who was engaged to a man who had turned her in to the authorities for being a Christian and promising her dowry to the poor if God would heal her sick mother. Since she was a Christian, they tried to burn her at the stake, but she wouldn't burn. The soldiers finally pierced her with a sword. She was considered the lady of light since she delivered food with candles on her head so as to see in the dark caves. This story was brought to the Swedes by missionaries in the 1700's during their famine years. The Swedes liked the story so much that they adopted her for their own and imagined the lady of light bringIng food to the hungry in Sweden during the famine. They said they could see her doing that in the early morning darkness. This has been carried down through the years and celebrated in schools, churches, hospitals, offices, and especially in homes where the oldest daughter is Lucia with younger daughters as her helpers and boys as star boys carrying a star on a pole to help light her way in the dark.

Swedes celebrate Christmas on Christmas Eve, eat Smorgasbord food, dance around the Christmas tree and then go to church for Julotta (Christmas Eve candlelight services.

Decorations on the tree consist of many straw-made ornaments, paper woven heart-shaped baskets to hold candy for the children, Swedish flags on a string and candles. They used to be real, but I suppose they have electric ones now like we have.

Scandinavian children put porridge out to feed Nisse, the Christmas buck. They also leave rice porridge for the tomptes (little elves) that help around the farm.

They, like several Scandinavian countries, take lanterns or candles to the graveyard at Christmas time.

They may put their trees out in the yard after Christmas with bread tied to the branches for the birds.

Then on King Knut's birthday, January 13th, they may take the trees to the center of town for a big bonfire and burn them all.

New Year is a time when all like to watch City fireworks. Swedes always love a party, so they may have a moose roast feast with warm mulled wine (called glogg) to drink.

SWEDISH SMORGASBORD MENU

Ham Swedish Meatballs Roast Moose or Deer
Boiled red-skinned new potatoes with parsley or dill
Rice Pudding with a hidden whole almond (for good luck or next single person is to marry within the year) served with Lingon berries and whipped cream
Pickled Herring Pickled beets Cucumbers in salt & vinegar water
Salads – as many as you want.
Brown sweetened beans with a cinnamon stick

Tuna Mold Pan Kaka Pudding Ost (cheese cake) Pudding served with Lingon

Potato Sausage Head Cheese lunch meat slices

Cabbage Rolls Smoked white fish, cold Deviled Eggs

Limpa Rye Bread Knacke bread (rye crisp) Swedish Coffee Bread

Butter balls Farmer's Cheese

Fruit Soup with whipped Cream

At least 7 kinds of cookies - Spritz, Drommar, Pepparkakar (gingerbread), Jam bars

Pecan tarts, Sugar Cookies, Finska Bars. Rosettes, Chocolate Brownies

Chapter twelve-St. Lucia
Day ~~12~~-13-1948
Marilyn @ Purdue University

Chapter Twelve – Sankta
Lucia today

Chapter Twelve
Midsummer Pole

Chapter Twelve - Christmas
at Mom & Dad's

CHAPTER THIRTEEN

Our Family Grew with Family and Animals

A. FAMILY

On my brother, Ralph's final stint in the Army, he was deployed to Okinawa, and was then transferred to Taiwan. He had been engaged to a girl in Massachusetts, but then he met and fell in love with Kathryn Huang in Taiwan. She had been working in the optical doctor's office where he went for new glasses.

When true love hits us, there's no stopping it. Our folks had suggested that if he still felt that way after coming home, he could send for her. Ralph knew that would be much more difficult to accomplish at getting her here later if they weren't already married, so he decided to surprise everyone and bring a bride home with him to the United States.

They married in Taiwan in April, 1961 and when he was discharged, they both came by ship. Kathy got really sick on the ship coming over and she thought she was really seasick. As it turned out, she was actually pregnant. Jacqueline Grace joined our family on March 13, 1962. She became quite an acomplished pianist and violinist due greatly to Kathy's encouragement and perseverance in being prolific in making sure Jackie was diligent in her practicing.

My folks sold the old homeplace on Center Street and bought a lot three blocks away and built a new house on Digby Road and moved in two weeks before Leon and my wedding. Leon and I married August 4, 1962 on mother's birthday. So next person to join our family was my new husband, Leon Fleeger.

After our lovely wedding, the second one in the new church at 1721 S. 9th St., we packed up my little green Nash station wagon I called "Sherbie", because it reminded me of lime sherbert. Each of my cars got names. My first car was an orange Volks Wagon beetle bug, so I called it my "Lady Bug".

We packed "Sherbie" to the ceiling with wedding presents and things we felt we needed to set up housekeeping, and set out for San Diego, California, making this our honeymoon. We traveled through Kansas City and Colorado visiting relatives along the way.

I was supposed to get a transfer job from Chicago, Ill. to San Diego. Ca. With GMAC and be able to work as soon as I got there. However, once we arrived, I found that there was no job waiting for me as promised. They also took their time in the Navy before they started to dispense my spousal pay to me as well.

We were kind of in dire straights in the beginning. We only had $500.00 left to start our new life far from our Indiana home.

We found a cute little apartment in a complex with a pool that was right outside our sliding glass doors. We kept hoping a job at GMAC would open up soon.

We got a small insurance check from my last job, and Leon gave blood as often as was allowed, and I got a small birthday check from the folks that we used to keep us in groceries. Thank goodness for the Naval commissary on the base which was much cheaper than a regular grocery store. I think we only paid forty cents for a gallon of milk and fifteen cents for a loaf of bread. It was unbelievable, and good even for 1962.

The next week the Navy finally came through with our stipend. See, God always comes through as long as we persevere and have patience and trust Him.

Then I finally got a job at GMAC in San Diego.

Leon kept surprising me in life. We had fourteen and a half wonderful years together with the joy of four beautiful healthy children.

The first surprise and disappointment was when he decided on his own without discussing it with me to move back to Lafayette when he finished his tour in the Navy. I had mentioned I wanted to stay in California and he decided he wanted to come back home to Lafayette. Guess he was homesick. I was disappointed at first, mostly because he didn't even discuss it with me. He sold our furniture, and had the Navy pack up all our things to ship to us in Indiana. At first we could not get jobs in Lafayette, so we ended up settling in Chicago. I got my job back at General Motors Acceptance Corporation and Lee decided to try to go to Wright Junior College to try to please me. He tried for a while, but college was really not for him.

OUR FOUR BLESSINGS

Our first little blessing was a girl, and that's what Lee really wanted. She was born in San Diego two days after our first anniversary on August 6, 1963. My Navy girlfriend told me I wouldn't like having a baby at the Naval hospital cause she said they just herd you through like cattle. Since I had very good medical insurance through General Motors, we opted for a regular doctor, and we only had a doctor bill of $25.00, so that was really good. No medical debt there. We got to go home on the third day, so the hospital bill was nothing. I believe I mentioned before that I drove myself first to the doctor's office and then on to the hospital, as Lee was aboard his ship. He made it before she was born though.

I was only at the hospital two and a half hours before she was born which was pretty quick for the first child especially since she was two weeks early on top of it. Leon wanted to name her "Annette" after the Mickey Mouse

Club character (Annette Funicello). I thought Yvonne sounded good as a second name and it was one of my favorite cousin's names from Kansas.

Mom and Dad came to California to meet their second granddaughter when she was a week old and they brought us back to Lafayette by car to meet the rest of the family for a visit. Leon was supposed to be getting out of the Navy in a couple of weeks and was supposed to come get us. The folks were thrilled with their two little granddaughters.

Since we ended up in Chicago, we settled in to a nice little homey neighborhood close to the Portage Park area close to the Covenant Portage Park church where we attended. We knew folks there as my uncle Kenny had been a minister there earlier on. We bought a three-apartment building on the quiet street of Grace Street near six corners shopping area. There was a nice little mom and pop grocery store on one corner and the grade school two blocks the other direction where Annette ended up going to kindergarten and first grade. I think it was called Gray School.

When Annette was three and a half, we were blessed with our second child. This cute little curly-headed blond boy came on February 13, 1966. He was born at Swedish Covenant Hospital in Chicago on Foster Ave. It was our denominational hospital associated with North Park College as well. He also came two weeks early. We were tickled to have one of each now and Annette was happy to have a little brother. I wanted to name this little six pound three ounce boy "Sean Patrick" since his father was Irish, but he wouldn't hear of it. My dad's middle name was Patrick, so I thought it would be nice for that reason too. We finally both settled on "Jeffrey Scott" and that was that.

He was born on a Sunday about the time the minister was giving his sermon on the television. In fact, the church was right across from the hospital. I was only in labor a couple of hours. He came to greet us at

12:12PM. I was anxious for my brother and sister-in-law to come visit their new nephew, but Swedish Covenant Hospital was so strict, they would only let the daddies in to visit.

I had a Bartlein cyst that had to be removed a month after Jeff's birth along with the Bartlein Gland too. To help it heal a nurse sprayed me with Americaine that I ended up being allergic to and I broke out in a burning rash all down my leg from the incision to my knee. Terribly painful!

Jeff was almost too beautiful to be a boy with his long curly eyelashes and curly hair and big dark blue eyes which I figured would be brown later- which they were.

Two days after he was born, I wrote a poem about my newborn son.

TO MY NEWBORN SON FEBRUARY 15, 1966

By Marilyn Sandberg Grenat

"To hear the words 'You have a new son'
Brought joy to our hearts and we felt we had won.

We counted the months and days
And we had nothing but praise.

Since the gender was a surprise till the end,
We only could give love and joy in a blend.

You're bone of our bone and flesh of our flesh,
But you're one of a kind coming all new and fresh.

You'll be a mix of Swedish and Irish
And you turned out to be quite a dish,

With blue eyes sparkling, a head full of curls.
Your sweet little mouth and long curly lashes- you're sure to attract the girls.

Babies are sweet and smell good too.
I better hurry and give you cuddles,
For it won't be long till you're out playing in the puddles.

Welcome to the Fleeger Home.
I hope it's not too soon that you roam."

Love, Your Momma

Jeff had an intrepid personality and was always adventurous and curious.

He attended and graduated from the same college that I did at North Park College in Chicago, Illinois, which is a University now.

While he was event planner, he met his wife, Joanna Neitzke at Hiatt Regency Hotel in Chicago in 2006 when he was forty. They were married In 2009 by a Captain on a boat on Lake Tahoe near the California line. Jeff got cancer in 2013 soon after our trip to Sweden, and he passed away in November, 2016 near Thanksgiving time. He was much too young to go at fifty, but had seven beautiful years with his lovely Joanna. He had the dreadful Lymphoma cancer with tumors in his abdomen that were very painful. They made him feel full and he wasn't able to eat, so basically was starved of nutrition.

My prayer pals of my Bible Study small group helped me get through those horrible three years. I spent some time with him in Arizona taking him to Phoenix to the Mayo Clinic there for his cancer treatments. They even tried stem cell transplants, which really didn't help either. They felt they could never do surgery to remove the tumors either.

Nothing seemed to help. No mother should ever have to go to any of their children's funerals. It's one of the most devastating experiences of my life, but my Heavenly Papa was a great comfort.

After losing both my beloved husband, Gene, to Alzheimer's six years before and my dear sweet only son, Jeff, to cancer, my therapy ended up being the result of my writing my first book - "Inspirations from the Heart" in 2018 that resulted in a poetry book.

Between 1966-1970, I had three miscarriages and that was hard to cope with.

On September 11, 1971, we were blessed with a third child that I thought could never happen. She was such a sweet miracle baby that we were so thrilled to receive. This little girl we named Kristina Amelia Elisabeth after my father's mother in Sweden. The Amelia part is after the aviator/ explorer and my aunt.

An old hometown doctor suggested an easy exercise for me to do during pregnancy that eliminated the danger of another miscarriage, and it worked. It worked again two years later as well when I got pregnant with our fourth blessing. Using the same method, I was able to deliver a second miracle baby girl that we named Jennifer Helen Michelle. Helen was after both of our Mothers. She came two years to the day after "Stina" on September 11, 1973.

Since we were now living in Lafayette, Indiana, they were both born at the old Home Hospital.

Since my mother had passed away in 1969, my Dad was very lonesome, so we moved from Chicago to Lafayette to be near him. We were able, by chance, to get to purchase our old homeplace on Center Street at a fairly reasonable price as the owners were going to move to Washington

D.C. Leon started with his brother to attempt to get into the plumbers' field. That job lasted just **a short** time until he got an opportunity about the time of Kristina's birth to get into the Lafayette Fire Department. My Father was able to help him there a bit and had put in a good word for him.

My Dad eventually contacted an old Swedish friend, Anna, he had known in Rockford, Illinois that had lost her husband about the same time he had lost our Mother. Since Dad had been pretty lonely without mom, he and Anna got close over several months and ended up marrying in August on my birthday (the 29th of August)., 1970.

When they decided to tie the knot, with none of our family invited except a couple of Welsh friends from our church, the Thomases, as witnesses in our small denominational chapel in our church proper by our minister.

I didn't have time to plan much, and not even time to invite Ralph and Kathy. I quickly, last minute, made a cake and had a small get together at my house after their ceremony to celebrate. It's what they wanted or all they would allow me to do. So our family, once again, was added to by Dad's new bride, Anna Wallgren, from Jamestown, N. Y.

In 1976, Leon came to me with the most devastating, unbelievable request I never thought I would ever hear. We had had some problems due to his deciding to take an interest in our flight instructor and his infidelity, but I never thought it would come to this. I begged him to go with me to a marriage counselor, but he would have no part of that. I guess he knew what they would tell him and he didn't want to hear that. In 1977, he insisted on a divorce. I finally consented after I realized he wasn't going to give up. His interest in the flight instructor increased but her interest in him waned.

We agreed on the details of how our property was to be divided and who would be responsible for certain financial obligations before we obtained the same attorney. I was to keep the children, the home we lived in and one car and he was to get the three apartment buildings and one car and keep those bills while I maintained the expense of our house. Lee was never very financial savoy, so I made it easy on him and only asked for about half the amount of child support, so I might be more apt to obtain it.

It's better to get an expected small amount regularly than not at all as I had seen in divorces through the court system. There were no concrete rules in the court system back then to help women, like being able to garnishee their wages if they didn't pay their child support like they have now. A woman really was at the mercy of hoping her ex-husband would honor his obligation to his family. By keeping the child support low, Leon always paid it even if it was sometimes a little late, but I could depend upon it. I had to take two jobs and sometimes three to meet all my financial obligations and put food on the table for the kids and myself as well as a roof over our heads.

School expenses, clothing, music lessons, for four kids, gas, utilities and any extras and I never took any government help except the cheese. There was never anything left over for a vacation or a treat like going out to eat. No pop or snacks like chips, etc. either. Just fruit and I would always make a balanced meal for them every evening. We were never hungry and always warm and most of all we stuck together and we loved one another. I brought the children up in church so they would know the Lord that always sustained us. They were good kids and I was always proud of them and am to this day. Even Leon complimented me on doing a good job, even though he wouldn't admit that necessarily to others.

Our divorce was final in the early part of 1977 after fourteen and a half years of marriage. I needed to find a job immediately in order to take care of the children and the only thing I could get within a day was a waitressing job at Howard Johnson's restaurant for $1.25 an hour. It was hard work. I eventually applied at the Sheriff's Department for an office job. It was a little more but still only $9, 250.00 a year in the mid seventies. It still wasn't enough to rear four children on even with the help of $3,000 a year in child support. It stretched the budget, but I made it work. Once in a while I would take a painting job or wallpaper job to help out on the weekends. I kept the waitressing job on top of the Sheriff's Dept. job for about six months.

Annette and my sister-in-law's occasional help tried to babysit the younger kids. I got the two younger girls in a nice church daycare after trying another first.

I worked under three different Sheriffs for fourteen and a half years. After about three years of struggling, with one job, I added a second job as custodian at our church evenings and Saturdays. I could take the two little girls with me to church and they would help me by dusting the pews and helping me clean the bathrooms and then they could nap on the couches in the foyer while I finished mopping and buffing the floors on two levels. I did this for ten years. It was a godsend for us even though it was usually only $43.00 a week. It bought us some food, and sometimes gas in the car.

I dated a few guys in latter 1977, but none of them really interested me. I was just concerned about raising my kids. About 1978, my sister-in-law, Ruth, introduced me to a guy named Vern and we dated for a while. He started to bug me about getting married saying he had lost his four kids and that he could help me raise my four children.

He was nice to me and bought a country home and another country lot close to town where he had this two-story house moved to the lot. He asked if I would help him fix it up and wanted me to wallpaper his living room. I really didn't feel like I loved him enough to marry him, but he kept on bugging me to marry him and said country living would be so nice for the children. He said we could have a nice big garden. He even came to church with me and just kept on how much he could teach Jeff, as he could do all kinds of things. He was always willing to help my dad too and he actually liked him.

He finally wore me down, so I asked the kids what they thought of the idea. I knew Jeff was the age where he really needed a male influence at age thirteen. The kids said, "Mom, what ever makes you happy, do it." So we finally decided on a wedding in the beautiful Purdue Horticulture Park under a big tree surrounded by lots of pretty flower gardens.

We didn't have a regular minister at the time as we were in between. I asked a local minister to marry us that had been in town for years and had been my counselor when I went through my divorce from Leon. We married on 7-21-79.

Just two or three months into the marriage I realized it might have been a big mistake, but I don't give up easily. I tried for quite a while to make it work, but Vernon changed in so many ways. He was verbally abusive to both me and the children. He stopped going to church with me and he became way too attentive to my seventeen-year-old daughter Annette. I was afraid to leave her alone with him when I was not home.

It came to a head one night when I was already asleep and his advances made Annette call her boyfriend in tears and he came out to get her and I awoke to a scuffle of him and Vern on the porch.

After that she went to live with her dad and his new wife, where problems were not a whole lot better. Vern got nasty with Jeff too and he ended up at his dad's as well. His wife's boys were always trying to get him in trouble and they and their mom told lies about him so that his dad would jump on him. Poor Jeff got a bum rap all the way around.

I had had enough of all of them and decided one day in February with snow ankle-deep, I was going to shovel that long country driveway and move out. I couldn't move to my Catula house that I had kept-thank goodness, because I had it rented out for a few more months. Leon had our old house back on Center Street and it was empty right now. It's hard to rent out in the winter, so I asked him if we could rent his house until my Catula house was empty. I said, "Your kids need a place to live, can we rent Center from you until my house is available?" I told him I couldn't pay what he was getting in rent, but I could pay what his mortgage was. We always tried to help one another out even though we were divorced. I think we were there about four months before going back to Catula. I'm just glad I had not sold it when I married Vern.

I think I lived with him about a year before I left, but I didn't jump into divorce for about six-nine months; at least I wasn't living with him. He kept trying to get me back, but I had had enough, and I knew he would never change. We finally divorced in 1981.

I was alone from 1981-1989. I left the Sheriff's Department in 1989 and went to work in the Accounting Department at Purdue University and was hired as an Accounting Supervisor. They had the same retirement plan, so I could combine the years.

In July, 1990, Kathy, my brother's wife, introduced me to an old high school classmate of Ralph's. She had sat next to him at Ralph's thirty-fifth high school class reunion dinner. When she found out he had just come back from working in California to his hometown and was looking for a nice Christian girl here, she jumped on it. She told him she had just the girl in mind for him, because she was thinking of me, and gave him my number. After he called me a couple of times, we decided to get together for dinner. We got close pretty quickly because at our age we were able to recognize a good combination and able to see we were good for each other with the same values, morals and good qualities. We were married on December 22, 1990. We were fortunate to have twenty wonderful great years together. His last eleven years he suffered from Alzheimer's and passed on April 3, 2010. We gain some and we lose some-such is life.

B. OUR ANIMALS-

In 1942 in Peoria, Illinois, we had a big brown dog we called "Dixie"/"Brownie" as Ralph remembered her and she had a litter of puppies that I remember jumping all over me at two and knocking me down and licking me all over my face so I couldn't get up until mother came to my rescue in the back yard.

In Sweden in 1946-7, I had a marvelous very smart, sweet cat that I called "Sippa" after the wild flower that grew in the woods. This little gray tabby cat followed me everywhere and would wait for me at the end of the lane every day at a certain time for me to get home from school. I loved her dearly and she learned to swim when Ralph flung her into a lake in the forest.

She was so smart and laid on her back to show mother her big wound in her stomach where another animal had taken a big bite out of her.

She cried so mournfully, that mother asked Ralph if he was tormenting Marilyn's cat again. "Oh no, Mother, I haven't touched her," he exclaimed. She knew to go let Mother know she was hurting.

Our third was brought home by Ralph to Center Street in Lafayette, In. around 1947. She was a cute little white Spitz mix with light tan ears. Ralph named her "Trixie" and she was with our family probably the longest until I was in college., about 1959. I had a black cat named "Cinder" and she had several litters of kittens. Then we had several dogs that never seemed to be quite trainable until Annette brought home the smartest, most beautiful collie I had ever seen. She named him "Rusty" and he was with us in two different houses. He lived quite awhile until the heart worms seemed to take him in spite of his getting treatments from the Veterinarian. We all loved that precious dog, but I think Jennifer took his loss the most. She came home from school one day and noticed he did not feel good and as she sat with him, he died with his head in her lap.

The next dog was a little reddish-brown Dachshund we named "Schatzie" which meant "darling" in German. He was a stray that came to us on Catula and we Took it to the pound. No one claimed him after three weeks, so Leon thought The children needed a dog, so he went back and got it and brought it to us.

Thanks a lot Leon!

Another animal to clean up after and another mouth for me to feed! I didn't get any help physically or monetarily either from him on that one either!

He would never come when you called him and if we took him for a walk, he'd get away from us and if he thought he could get away, he would run and make you chase him. When we caught up with him he'd make us pick him up and carry him back home. He was sweet, but a pain in the patooty. He finally got out one day when I was gone and ran away. We found him at the pound again, but some one else fell in love with him and wanted to adopt him, so I let them. It was a little older lady from out of town and I thought they might be a good fit for one another.

I acquired several cats from the kids who couldn't keep them, so we had a couple from Annette. One was "Sydney" and one was "Smokey" or something like that.

Kelsey wanted a little white kitten that one of my tenant's cat's had, but when she got it home, her mom wouldn't let her keep it, so I acquired that one, and had her for nearly fifteen years before I had to have her put to sleep. Kelsey named her "Lulu" and she became my buddy and pal and would meet me at the door at night just like a little dog.

I love animals, but when Corrine wanted me to get another little cat or dog to keep me company, I didn't feel it was a good idea for fear they may outlive me, and then it might be a problem for someone to take them over if I die.

It's a lot of expense and responsibility to take care of an animal, and a bother to others if I ever would want to go anywhere, so I've opted out of getting another little pet. I am done with having pets at this stage of my life even though they have been a joy in the past.

Chapter Thirteen-Pets
Dixie

Chapter Thirteen – Pets
Trixie

Chapter Thirteen-Pets
Trixie & Sippa

Chapter Thirteen-Pets
Cinder my Cat

CHAPTERTHIRTEEN
LULU CAT

Chapter Thirteen
Smokey

Chapter Thirteen- Annettte's
H. S. Graduation & Rusty

Schatzie – our Dachshund

Lulu -my cat for 14 Years

CHAPTER FOURTEEN

Trips & Excursions With Family Skiing

1960- Ralph and I cross-country skied all the time in Sweden when we were younger, but downhill skiing was not my forte. When we lived in Chicago in the 1960's, Ralph and Kathy wanted me to go with them and take Annette and Jeff up to Wisconsin to go downhill skiing. Those were big hills and I never mastered doing the plow to stop. The day we went it was a bit icy too. I didn't even know how to slow down, so when I got half way down, and I realized how icy it was, I thought, "Wow, how am I going to stop at the bottom?" Am I going to have to hit that fence to stop? As I got closer, all I could think of was to just sit down, so I did. When Kathy said, "Do you want to go up again?" I said, "No thank you, I don't think this sport is for me!" I thought I was lucky not to break any bones. It always looks so fun, but nothing is fun you haven't learned how to do properly. That was the end of my skiing. After all, didn't Sonny Bono die running into a tree while skiing? I thought I better stay on the flat ground or a sled if I was going to go on a snowy hill.

SKYDIVING

In 2015 on my seventy-fifth birthday I decided to do some fun bucket list thing, so my twenty-four year old granddaughter, Kelsey, and I made up our minds to go together since no one else seemed brave enough to want to go with us. We had wanted to try it for a while, so off we went to Indy Skydiving in Frankfort, Indiana. It was considered one of the safest places to do this in the midwest.

It was August 29, 2015, and John and Tina came to watch us. Kelsey had a para trooper from Russia, and I had a paratrooper from Greece to go with me tandem, so we felt pretty safe. No one else seemed brave enough to go. I even bought some special jumping boots to protect my weak ankles. I had broken one ankle twice before with three breaks in one. There probably was no stress anyway, as the top tandem guy is the one who puts his feet down and all we had to do was hold our legs out straight and sit down, so we had no stress on our ankles. it's quite easy actually. They don't let anyone go alone unless they've had training and jumped many times. We, prior to the jump, viewed a video and the trainers told us what to do. We wore goggles to protect our eyes, the instructor, top tandem guy wore the parachute. We had a freefall for a few moments and it felt free like we were a bird. When he pulled the cord on the chute, we slowed down a bit. We had hired a videographer to take some pictures both by video and also some still pictures. They are fun to have. In fact, I used one still picture for my next Christmas card. Folks were shocked that I did that at that age, but I think President Bush did it at an even older age. It was exhilarating to say the least and I'm so glad I did it. So is Kelsey. It was quite the thrill of a lifetime.

In September of 1990 I had just turned fifty, and since Jeff worked for Delta Airlines as an agent right out of college, he thought it would be nice to take his mom on a trip to Hawaii for her 50th birthday celebration. It was so exciting to be planning such an elegant trip to such a gorgeous destination.

Annette had been there before and she always knew how to plan trips to be fulfilling and exciting. She gave us lots of tips on what to do and what to see.

We went to two Islands and stayed several places. One of them was at our friends-the Mills' condo they had on Waikiki Beach for a few days. We got a new Hotel for a few days for a fantastic price since Jeff was in the travel business, as a trial so he could recommend them to other travelers. It was a $300.00 a night room that we got for $25.00 instead.

We went to a factory that made exotic Hawaiian clothing and I bought a sundress for me and a matching shirt for Gene in lovely pastel flowers.

We toured the Dole plantation where they grew pineapples. I was so dumb, I thought they grew in trees like coconuts, but was surprised to see that they grew on the ground like pumpkins.

We attended two luaus and had roasted pig in the ground that was really delicious. We watched authentic Hawaiian dancers do their native dances. It was quite a show.

Finally, Jeff said one day, "Mom you have so many things planned, but I would like to go to the beach and get a sun tan for a few days. So he went to the beach while I went shopping. There were so many interesting shops there.

When we went to Lahini, we saw and held tame parrots on our arms right on the beach. That was cool. We had so much fun and lots of good food while we were there for nine days.

Jeff even had time to take some scuba diving lessons in the ocean where his instructor got some neat deep sea pictures of him. He really enjoyed that as he was very adventurous.

This is one trip with my son I will always remember and cherish.

In 1996, Jeff was working in Finland as a second language English teacher to Finnish post high school students for one and a half years. They wanted an American who couldn't speak Finnish to teach American English to the students. He really loved being in Finland and got acquainted with quite a few people. One of his closest friends of the town near Nurmes where he taught was the town mayor, and they would go fishing together a lot.

When his teaching job was over, he was thinking about staying. The only way he could do that was to get another job. He was having his 30th birthday while there and I was afraid if he stayed, I might not get to see him for a long time. I didn't want him to be alone for his birthday, so I bought a ticket to go see him in February for his birthday. There was lots of snow and it was very cold. In fact, frost formed in the air and on my hair.

He took me all around to see where his school was where he taught. Then he went on an interview at Nokia for a job while I was there. He didn't get it, so I was secretly happy about that, because I really wanted him to come back to the States.

He was living in an apartment in Helsinki at the time. We were invited to a friend of his out in the countryside for dinner. I believe she was the mayor's sister.

After we got off the train, we had to walk in fairly deep snow quite a ways into The forest to get to her house. She had a cute little house in the woods that reminded me of a Hans Christian Anderson fairy tale setting. She had two girls, but otherwise was alone, so Jeff had helped by doing a few repairs around her house for her.

Jeff eventually came home after his visa was up and started working for a travel company that catered to CEOs of Fortune 500 companies. After working for BI for awhile, he started his own company doing the same thing. He called it Eventures, Inc. He did that for about twenty years or so before he passed.

His adventures took him over the years to about eighty countries. He also was very adventurous and loved to climb mountains and even went to the top of Kilimanjaro in Africa.

While he worked in those travel jobs, he met his wife, Joanna, who was an event planner too for big name brand Hotels. Jeff met her at Hiatt Regency Hotel in Chicago, Illinois in 2006 when he was forty. They were married in 2009 on Lake Tahoe by the Captain of a boat in a lovely wedding. They were married about seven years before he passed of Lymphoma cancer on November 26, 2016 when he was only fifty- much too young to die. They lived in the Tucson, Arizona area.

Besides mountain climbing, Jeff had done bungee jumping off a bridge, yak riding, running with the bulls in Spain, and toured Europe with a friend by foot after completing a "Student Abroad" program for a semester in Sweden via North Park College. His intrepid personality made him never afraid to try anything.

I think we might have been made from the same cloth, so to speak, as some of his nerve might have come from me. Both my husband, Lee, and I wanted to learn how to fly a plane, so we bought a four-seater Cessna and kept it at Purdue University airport where the flight students could rent our plane for their lessons.

Their renting of our plane made the payments for our plane. We also took our lessons there. It was quite a thrill to learn how to fly. It allowed us a few trips that we otherwise would not have been able to participate in. Lee got to be a pretty good pilot and even did some glider flying. I never wanted to try that, because I thought it was too scary to be up there without an engine and just relying on the wind. He flew a lot more than I got to, because it got to be too expensive.

The money we had set aside for my lessons got used up by Leon, so I never got my license as you had to have enough hours and solo time that I never got. I still could fly with Leon though and often flew the plane while he slept, but I'd just have to wake him up when we got home to land the plane.

In 2013 Jeff and I went to Sweden on a trip and when we got home he discovered that he had cancer, so we were so glad that we got to take that trip. He only survived for three more years, and passed around Thanksgiving of 2016. We got to visit about 50 cousins, several cities and stayed in a little cottage at the famous Gullen Gottern resort on Lake Vattern. We visited my grandfather's village, Haurida, where I went to first grade, Huskvarna, where some of my cousins live, Stockholm, Uppsala, Gothenburg, where my sister lives, and Lund, where another cousin lives. We toured the castle and watched the changing of the guards and were fascinated as they now have some female guards. We toured a bit of Lund University where my cousin, Magnus Lagnevik, was a professor. We also scoured the whole island of Visingso where a lot of Vikings were buried. Not too long ago they had no cars on that island, but only horse-drawn wagons for transportation.

They do allow cars now though and folks can take their cars over by ferry from Granna. We also checked out a 300 year-old church and a 900 year old church on the island.

Jeff had had his picture taken in 1975 by a big wooden statue giant in Granna, so he wanted that same pose taken again in front of that same giant thirty-eight years later. So we have the two, and they are fun to compare.

In 2020 I was going to take my middle daughter, Stina, to Sweden so she could see from where her roots were from. She was the last of my four children who had never been to Sweden. Then the Covid pandemic hit us and we couldn't go then. Annette and Jeff had been in 1975, Jenni had been in 1984 with grandma & grandpa for four months, and Jeff went again to college a semester on the student-abroad program, and again with me in 2013, so it was still Stina's turn to go.

We finally got to go for Midsummer Festivities in June of 2022. Now I can rest easy knowing that they all have been and enjoyed the experience. We were only able to be there a week, but we crammed in four major cities and visits to about forty cousins. It was a whirlwind trip, but lots of fun to see my relatives one more time. My time before 2013 was 1992 when I took my folks for Christmas which was different, because we always went otherwise during the summer months.

Dad was happy to get to go one last time, but sadly on Christmas Eve, just two days before we were to go home, he had a heart attack and he and Ann had to stay an extra six weeks in the hospital and a rehab nursing home before he could come home. We hired a nurse to accompany them home on the plane and we got an ambulance from Chicago to Lafayette, Indiana Home Hospital. He was ninety years old, and he only lasted three days at home, but he was happy that he got to see everybody and got to be buried next to his first wife, Helen, our mom.

In 2009 we got to go to Lake Tahoe on a yacht to Jeff and Joanna's wedding that was really fun and quite unique and beautiful. The Captain married them on the boat.

John, Tina, & Corrine took me with them on a cruise to the Bahamas and Grand Turks in October, 2018. That was very interesting and fun. I had never been on a recent fancy cruise ship except for the old Drottningholm in 1946-1947 and the Kungsholm in 1954 across the Atlantic Ocean to Sweden. Those were nice but not as fancy as the newer ships.

In 1960, the folks and I got to fly for the first time to Sweden after my graduation from college and dad always rented a car once we got there. I wanted to see a few other countries since they were close to each other. We went to Norway from Sweden, Finland, Germany, Denmark, the

Netherlands, Holland, France, and Belgium. We changed planes in England and Iceland, but didn't see much of the last two countries. We drove through the other countries and saw quite a bit of them.

I have been so very lucky to have gotten to see as much of the world as I have. You would think dad would not want to drive on vacation since he drove so much on his traveling job. It was lucky he didn't mind driving, so he took the family some place around the States every summer and would try to get in some educational spots along with the fun of visiting family. They are all good memories he helped make for us.

I'm thinking one more thing I would like to do on my bucket list is go up in a balloon ride in a basket. I don't think there are any around near here, so I may never get that accomplished. Gene and I took Corrine, our granddaughter, up in one at Conner Prairie a few years back when she was four or five, but it was tethered so it didn't go far – just up and then back down. I want to go some place where a pilot has to be present. It was fun but not as adventurous as it could have been. I've since heard that those rides are pretty expensive though, so that may be another reason I probably won't get to do it.

Chapter Fourteen -Trip to Hawaii-Sept. 1990 Pearl Harbor

Aloha From Hawaii

Chapter Fourteen – Jeff & Marilyn's trip to Hawaii on her 50th birthday-9-1990

Chapter Fourteen-Trips 2013- Renovation of Grandpa Sandberg's old house from yellow to traditional Swedish red.

GRANDPA SANDBERG'S HOUSE

Chapter Fourteen-Skydiving Trip 2015 on Marilyn's 75th birthday with Kelsey

Skydiving on 8-29-15 on Marilyn's 75th birthday

CHAPTER FIFTEEN

My Third Husband – Bernard "Gene" Grenat 1990-2010

Jeremiah 29:11 "For I know the plans I have for you, declares the Lord, 'Plans to prosper you and not to harm you, plans to give you hope and a future.'

"Hebrews 11:40 "God had planned something better for us so that only together with us would they be made perfect."

I Corinthians 13:4 a "Love is patient."

Ecclesiastes 3:1 says "To everything there is a season, and a time to every purpose under the heaven." We felt this was our season to be happy.

Gene Grenat wrote this poem for Marilyn Sandberg Fleeger (during this time) to give her upon her return from Hawaii where she went with her son, Jeff, for her birthday celebration.

Poem "I Am Waiting" September 12,1990

(Poem of Love for Marilyn)

For a niche in your armor to
Appear and say you are less than
Angelic and are still a struggling mortal.

For the first time my mind and body are not
Willing to leave all other interests behind and
Rush to be with you under any pretext.

For the feeling to hug and kiss you
At all times I am with you, to
Become less than desperate.

For this state of awe to be
Replaced with a knowledge
<u>My prayers for a wonderful</u>
<u>Mate have been answered.</u>
For proof Male and Female
True Virgos can't be <u>Perfect</u>
<u>Marriage partners</u> as well.

For this string of absolutely
Astounding sameness of feelings
And views to end and indicate a
Less than amazing agreement
Between us.

For you to have a great time in
Hawaii with Jeff and return
With a sense of missing me."

Lovingly, Gene
By Bernard 'Gene' Grenat

Since Kathy introduced Gene and me in July, 1990 and we realized we were perfect for one another, after dating for six months, we decided to marry on December 22, 1990. I know some thought it was too soon, but when you know it's right and you're a good fit, there's no use wasting any time in enjoying life together.

Before we met, you might say he was a male chauvinist and I might as well have been called a female chauvinist. I didn't feel superior to the opposite sex, I just didn't feel too kindly toward them. I felt as though I had been wronged by them far too many times and felt like they felt they were superior to our female gender. We had both been kind of against the opposite sex because of our undesirable former experiences. We knew what a perfect desirable candidate should look like, but never thought there were any of those left and available. I think the good Lord was looking out for both of us and meant for us to find one another. I'm not saying that we were perfect, because no one is, but we knew we were very compatible.

We found we had lots of similar interests and likes. First of all, we both loved our Lord and Savior and wanted to please Him in our relationship and friendship.

Gene wanted to show me respect and affection in a Christian way. He decided he would not kiss me on our first three dates as he said he didn't want to mess our association up or scare me away by being too forward. He showed me great respect and courtesy and was a perfect gentleman.

We ended up being together every day after July and August. Jeff took me to Hawaii in September for nine days for my fiftieth birthday and Gene told his mom how hard he had fallen for me while I was gone. He ended up writing the poem for me at the beginning of this chapter that said how he felt we were a perfect match as mates. His mom said she knew he was in love with me by how much he missed me while I was gone.

We dated from July to December and decided we wanted to be a pair and planned our wedding for December 22, 1990.

He was always so respectful of my kids too and never tried to be their dad. He felt they had one of those and he just wanted to be their friend, which they really respected. They really liked Gene and were very happy for me and our happiness.

In another year, Jennifer was gone from home too, as Tina and John had gotten married a week before we did and were off to school at Vincennes, In. Jenni moved to Ohio and learned to fine-tune her manicurist abilities. As a trained Cosmetologist, she desired this phase the most and wasn't as happy at cutting hair. She became quite proficient at that and started her own manicure and pedicure business when she moved back to Lafayette. She had quite a successful business for about ten years. When she decided to close that business and go into another one, her clients were extremely disappointed. She does still do this for some people today though that are able to convince her. For instance, she treats her mother to this art once or twice a month.

Jenni met Brett that she ended up marrying and she felt at her age she should have medical insurance which she didn't feel she could afford having her own business. She got an opportunity to work for a title company as a title closer and she became quite proficient at that and was in great demand by several title companies. She was in that business for nearly twenty years, but it was very stressful and demanding even though she got the insurance she had been wanting.

She got to know a builder through her title job and got an opportunity to work for this prominent well-known builder. As with any new job, there was much to learn, but she loves it and it's a lot less stressful and she gets to go home on time every evening.

Her first husband and she departed and divorced after a few years, but she found her beloved soul mate, Bob, and he and Jen have been married since 2009.

In fact it's a joy to see all of my children happily married. My oldest daughter, Annette after a divorce to her first husband found her sweet mate, Dave, and is happily married since 2001.

Daughter number two, Kristina, has been married to John since June, 1991 (December, 1990). They have seen many wonderful years together.

Jeff only got seven years with his lovely Joanna before cancer took him in November of 2016.

It has been such a joy to see all of my kids happily married and they all love getting together and have a wonderful time. They even go on vacations sometimes together.

Tina and Annette are both Dental Hygienists.

Gene and I had twenty wonderful years together before complications of the Alzheimer's took him. We always enjoyed the kids and grandchildren together before he passed. He had Alzheimer's for the last eleven years of his life and I had to leave my Purdue University job in 2003 to take care of him until he passed in 2010. The last four months were spent at the Veterans Home which he wanted to do. It got a bit difficult to keep him contained at home even with door alarms and a GPS bracelet. I was afraid he'd get out and possibly get hit or harmed.

Gene was always so patient with me and always wanted to go with me wherever I went, but he didn't want to go into the stores and walk around as he had bursitus in the hip. If I didn't take the keys with me, he sometimes would forget he was waiting for me and might drive off which he did on several occasions.

One time when I went to the material store to get patterns and material for a dress I wanted to make for my son's wedding, I told him he'd be bored, but he still wanted to go with me. He stood by so patiently waiting for me to take my time picking out all of my selections and a couple of ladies there took notice. They asked, "My goodness, is he always that patient?" I said, "Yes he really is."

They wanted to take him home with them so he could teach their husbands how to be patient like that. I told them I couldn't spare him.

I asked him one time how he happened to get so patient and he said that he worked at it. Bless his heart! I tried to be patient with him like he was with me, but it wasn't always easy, especially with his antics having Alzheimer's.

One day when we were working together in the yard, I kind of lost it. I was raking leaves together and putting them in a basket and bringing them from one side of the house to the other side to Gene and he was dumping them over the fence down into the ravine. He did fine for a while, but all of a sudden he dumped back in the front yard instead of throwing it over the fence. I felt so bad that I had lost my patience. I just was surprised he did that, because he had been doing it perfectly before. He couldn't help it; he just got confused. Alzheimer's does crazy things to the mind. I will always remember and miss his patience and love to me. It's a big learning process for the caregiver to know how to act and react quickly with patience with an Alzheimer's patient. There's a big hole in my heart with him gone. In retrospect I wish I had been a quicker learner.

~~Chapter Fifteen~~ MyThird Husband-Gene Grenat 1990-2010

CHAPTER SIXTEEN

Grandchildren & Great Grandchildren

It's always exciting to hear you're going to be a grandparent let alone a great grandparent.

The thought of a new little person coming into the family is thrilling for everyone. They develop their own little personalities very quickly and become a pure joy.

We have kept all of my girls' kids from time to time. I basically took care of Corrine soon after birth until she went to kindergarten. I ran a daycare group for several children besides her as well. I originally looked after Kelsey and Emily before that occasionally as well. These were my grandchildren. Now it's my joy to care for their children.

I had the fortune of another granddaughter, Kandace Delong, through my daughter Jenni's second husband, Bob. She was born of his first marriage and now she's graced us with an added blessing.

I was lucky enough in 2021 to be expecting three new little great grandchildren. One came in June - a boy, one in July – a girl, and one in August – another girl. They were all cousins and we realized Christmases would be gloriously fun and probably hilarious with three one-year old plus toddlers. They were definitely pandemic babies. It was a rough year with the covid virus and folks stayed home a great deal more.

Obviously, these three great grandbabies were from my grandchildren. My oldest, Annette, had one son – Owen who was the daddy of a little boy on June 31st that they named River. I never ever heard him cry.

He was the happiest baby that smiled constantly. He was the spitting image of his daddy when he was little. He advanced so quickly that he took his first steps at ten months and was running by his first birthday. His mommy, Paige, had the cutest first birthday party for him with the Mickey Mouse theme. He had a Mickey Mouse costume from head to toe. He enjoyed a "smash cake" that he dove into with both hands. His cousins came too. There were aunts and uncles, friends and grandparents as well. There was lots of fun and good food had by all.

The next little great grandchild – Charlotte, was born on July 26th to Tina's oldest daughter, Kelsey. She looked older than a newborn because she had a full head of dark hair with big brown eyes. So cute! Her mom had fun putting little pony tails in her hair. She was a smiley one too!

After several weeks Kelsey's sister, Emily, had my third great grandchild of the year on the 18th of August. She, Sylvia Diane, looked like a typical little Sweden and a lot like Emily did as a baby. Blonde curly hair with BIG blue eyes made her the opposite of Charlotte. These two little girls will wow the boys and their fathers will probably have to beat the guys off with a stick! They will grow up to be the best of friends. Charlotte started walking at a year and Sylvia took her first steps at day care at fourteen months.

Since Emily's husband, Jeff, recently got hired as a Sheriff's Deputy in another county, he had to move to that territory. While they were selling their current home, they temporarily stayed with Em's sister before they were able to find and buy their new home in the county he was going to be working in.

Thus the two little cousins lived with each other for a short time before they reached a year of age. One if their great grandmothers, me, was watching them three days a week at their home.

That was such a joy for me to be with them and the girls were not only lucky to get to be together to get to know one another, but also to get to have someone their own age to play with. They would jabber together and sound like they were really carrying on a conversation. It was so sweet to watch them interact.

I see Charlotte's big brother, Harrison, who is four years old, but there are some great grandchildren I never see from Gene's side of the family. There is one in Colorado and one here in town. Gene has grandchildren from California and another that I have no idea where they are, because none of them have kept in contact with me since their grandpa passed. Some of them didn't even keep in contact with him. In fact, I never even hear from his daughter either.

The only family members I hear from on his side are his son, a sister, & a sister-in-law. Once in a blue moon I will hear from a nephew. It's very sad when family members desert you, but it's their choice. It gets a little old when I have to be the only one reaching out. I never would want to force anyone to feel like they had to contact me.

My blood grandchildren and great grandchildren are wonderful to keep in contact with me and they fill my heart with joy.

Chapter Sixteen-Grandson Owen & Paige Patrick & River - 2021

Chapter Sixteen -Granddaughter Emily & Jeff Zanker & Sylvia-2021

Kandace Delong

CHAPTER SEVENTEEN

Girl Friends & Boy Friends 1946-2022

Proverbs 17:17 "A friend loves at all times."

Proverbs 18:24 "A friend sticks closer than a brother."

Poem: By Marilyn Sandberg Grenat

"A True Friend"
"A true friend he always is
And I have no doubt to wonder about.

He is special in all he does.
He cared for his Mom,
And that could never be a bomb.

When I need him,
He is always at the brim.

He comes to assist,
And I never need to insist.

No matter how small or large the task,
He comes along without a mask.

He covers all the problems
That he can sufficiently solve them.
If I need roofing, electronics, or a picture hanging,
He is there with banging.

A hammer or a drill -
He always comes with skill.
My friend Don is always golden
With much expertise he is bold in.

It's nice to have a friend
That in which we can always depend.

Thanks to the reliable friend
We can always count on in the end."

My girl friends started in Sweden with my best friend being another foreign student in first grade. Her name was Perico from Finland. During WWII, Sweden being neutral, offered protection to Finnish children by allowing them to come to live with Swedish families to keep them protected from the war. Perico lived with my grandfather's neighbors, the Gustafsons. We had fun at school in the small village of Haurida while we went to a one-room schoolhouse. It wasn't long after that that Perico disappeared. Perhaps she went back to Finland to her family as many did. Some decided to stay though and become Swedish residents. Some of my cousins took some Finnish children in and raised them as their own and even adopted them. Tuovi was one of my cousins that was from Finland. One year when we visited her as an adult – I think it was 1992, she had a wonderful moose roast dinner for us. It was magnificent! We had visited her in Colorado when she was there working as a maid for an affluent family too. I have since lost her connection and I really regret that, as she and her family were so much fun.

Sometimes we lose contact with friends and family and we wonder if that's smart.

When my folks brought us back to the United States to Lafayette, Indiana, in 1946, we moved to 1418 Center Street and my next door neighbor was Holle. The girl on one corner was Judy and a friend around the corner on 15th Street was Ann. We all had so much fun together. Shirley lived across the street too and we all played the neighborhood games typical of the day.

When the fourth of July fireworks were set off at the Columbian Park, three blocks away, we would go to the corner and sit on Maple's hill to watch them.

As we got older, Clydette, a couple of blocks away on Alabama Street, became my friend. Eventually in high school, I met Judi across the street and we became such good friends that we became like sisters. She was dating a boy from Klondike named Jerry. He introduced me to his best friend Marvin, so we dated together for a period of time. They were famers that went to Klondike high school, and were very sweet. Marvin knew my religion was very important to me and he offered to leave his Catholic religion and give up smoking as well. I respected him enough to tell him he didn't need to change anything he did for me.

We both went our separate ways eventually, as I knew he wasn't really for me.

Jerry ended up marrying Judi and they had three girls and a boy. The first was Todd, and Judi made me his godmother. That was so sweet even though I was so young. Judi's little brother, Jimmy, always called me "Minnie Mouse".

Judi and I remained close as sisters through the years. They first lived in Crawfordsville, In. and then moved to Florida. Judi & Jerry divorced and eventually Todd and his mother lived in Largo, Florida. Even though Judi has now passed on, Todd and I still keep in contact. I love that kid!

My friends, Ann and Judy have also passed away too. I think Holle is still in the near vicinity, but I'm not sure about the rest of the girls.

There are still some of my male friends around. Chuck was my freshman friend from high league youth group at church, and still goes to our church. He was the one that introduced me to my first husband, Leon. Leon is also gone now, but I still see Chuck at reunions and church.

Danny was a friend I met at Covenant Harbor Bible Camp from Galesburg, Illinois. He even went to North Park College like Ralph and I did.

When I was almost fourteen, I met a seventeen-year-old, Willy, who was from Germany and was a lot of fun to know. He was a steward aboard the M.S. Gripsholm ship that my dad and I took across to Sweden in 1954. There are many different friends we can meet in life and then lose track of but are very interesting to get acquainted with.

I did meet a couple of former classmates recently for a brief period which was interesting, but very brief.

I am perfectly okay alone, because I love my full life completely. I don't feel I need relationships to complete me.

After Chuck introduced Leon and me, we dated for six years before we decided to get married. Leon had been in the Navy for three years by then, and when he asked me to marry him, I thought being a Navy wife in California might be fun.

We lived there his last year in the Navy and had our first child in San Diego, California. Then we moved to Chicago, Illinois, where we lived from 1963-1970. After my mother passed away in 1969, we realized that we should probably move to Lafayette, Indiana in 1970 to be close to my lonely dad. Leon and I divorced in 1977. I was married briefly from 1979-1981 to Vern and then divorced.

I was alone from 1981-1990. I didn't date much then as I wanted to devote mytime to my last two girls at home.

After meeting my true soulmate in July, 1990, I married Bernard "Gene" Grenat. We were happily married for twenty years before complications from Alzheimer's took him. I dated a couple of guys after that but never changed my marital status for the next thirteen years. And I don't expect to change that either any time soon or ever.

Chapter Seventeen-Perico
Finnish Friend 1946

Chapter Seventeen - Friends
Willy – 1954 aboard Ship

Chapter Seventeen – Friends
Danny, Rita, & Bill 1957
Galesburg, Ill.

Chapter Seventeen-Friends
Ed the Painter – 1976

Lafayette, Indiana
Chuck Lowrey – 1960
USAF Before going to
France

CHAPTER EIGHTEEN

Love And Lessons Learned

I John 4:11
"Since God so loved us we also should love one another."

I John 4:19
"We love because He first loved us."

Unconditional love means no matter what happens to us, we should love everybody. God, therefore, could have been saying, "Love everyone, and I will sort them out later."

My poem "LOVE EVERYONE" by Marilyn Sandberg Grenat 10-21-2022

"Love everyone as we should,
Just as God knew we could.

After all isn't that what the apostle John said,
And the better we understand that, the quicker we'll be ahead.

It's not always easy to forgive,
But if we do, we'll be on the right road to live.

God gave us the perfect example of perfection
And we now know how to show our affection.

As God loved us, we also should love one another.
Love completely – just like a mother."

Another Poem by Marilyn Sandberg Grenat

"SMART REMARKS"

"Sometimes we can think we only know the best.
But if we're not willing to listen to others,
We can miss out on good advice from the rest.

Sometimes we want to do all the talking,
So we show lots of balking.

You don't have to all their advice follow,
But pick and choose some good advice to swallow.

An emergency room technician was keen and discovered my son's tumors,
That a doctor didn't bother to investigate or even humor.

My sister-in-law taught me good eye exercises,
And it gave me great surprises.

Others gained from this and now don't need glasses,
And now she at eighty still wears no glasses.

Doctors prescribed all kinds of creams for rashes,
But my old stand-by – A&D ointment – healed with no clashes.

Drugs can sometimes do good but sometimes have worse
Side affects than the original problem.

So if you can find food or a natural solution,
Please take heed and use instead of giving your body polution.

I'm allergic to most antibiotics
But learned early on to fight infections with vitamin E.
That has given me so much glee.

Don't dismiss all that you think is rotten advice,
As you can yourself decide what advice is nice.

So others' suggestions can sometimes us save,
So you can decide whether to disregard or rave.

My cholesterol statins gave my muscles the fits,
As the ER doctor told me it was the pits.

I discovered a natural cholesterol support
(red yeast rice) through my natural vitamin company report.

I could hardly hold a glass of water
With the old statin meds that me would slaughter.

With all my natural medical advice in books,
I soon learned other ways to beat the crooks."

I always was happy with my earthly mother and father and always felt they loved one another and my brother and me. However, if I might have sometimes been upset with them, I knew there was a heavenly Father I couldalways count on without fail. He is a constant, reliable, loving papa that always makes me feel loved no matter what. What a comfort. I know without fail that He will forgive, understand and love me unconditionally.

On the other hand, my husband always said he didn't have that from hisearthly father, but he had come to an understanding that it really didn't matter so much, as he knew his heavenly Father was everything to him that he craved and wanted. What a realization for one to come to and with such acceptance.

I think some of us sometimes have difficulty in realizing and accepting this. many feel they have done so many wrongs in life that no one could ever forgive or love them the way our Heavenly Papa does.

But He does and I can't impress upon you enough how completely true that is. It may be difficult to realize how anyone could love another no matter what they've done in life, but our Heavenly Father and Jesus Christ forgives and loves all. Wow! Isn't that amazing?! Let it soak in and try to accept it. How can we not trust and appreciate that?! I'm so grateful my Christian parents knew and taught me that.

While my parents always showed me love and acceptance, I'll never forget one time when my mother thought I had done something wrong, but I had not. I don't even remember what the deed was. Since I always wanted to please my mother, I thought I should admit it so she wouldn't be so mad at me. I pictured she'd forgive me and then give me a hug. She surprised me and looked at me sternly and said, "Well, just don't do it again!" There was no hug nor forgiveness. I thought, man maybe I shouldn't have admitted the wrong deed. Now, I realize she was just human and felt she was doing her earthly proper duty as a good mother. I have never forgotten this. Perhaps I'm too sensitive a person. However, lesson learned is this: earthly parents are just human, but our Heavenly Father always forgives, but still disciplines.

Even a big brother can teach a younger sister something. And this was when we were all grown up. I thought we were always taught to be grateful for something when it was given to us. Not only in my receiving but also my giving. I can't even remember the gift or deed I did for someone, but I thought it was only common courtesy or good manners and my right to expect a simple "thank you" in return? When I was discussing this with my brother, the next thing out of his mouth surprised me, but it made me stop and think. He said, "When you do or give something to someone, it should never be with the idea of the need to have a returned thanks. It should be done with a giving open heart without any expectations!" Wow! Since our parents had taught us good manners, I thought it was just fine to expect a "thank you" back for a good gesture. As Christians, he was trying to impress upon me, that we should not "need" that and not "expect" that in order for all to be proper or acceptable. That's a true giving Christian heart! We can give without ever expecting something in return.

My poem 11-21-2019

"A LESSON LEARNED FROM MY BROTHER"

By Marilyn Sandberg Grenat

"A lesson a day I have learned,
We should not give with the thought of something in return.

Our hearts should be overflowing,
With generosity ever glowing.

Give out of love,
And our blessings will come from above.

Thank you Jesus and Ralph for opening my eyes,
And 'no thanks' will I not despise."

My dad taught me a lesson in honesty when I was very, very young – about eight or so. We had just come home from a trip to the drugstore. He discovered that the clerk had given him two extra cents in her change to him. He said, "We have to go back to give it to her so her drawer won't be short." I thought that was a little strange for just two cents, but I feel Daddy was trying to teach me a lesson in honesty no matter how little it was.

When I was grown and worked in Accounting and as a cashier in Chicago at General Motors Acceptance Corporation, there was one other cashier who had made a large mistake and accidentally given five hundred dollars extra back to a customer who was making a car loan payoff. When she discovered the mistake at the end of the day, she called him up to mention the mistake in hopes he would bring the $500.00 back. He said, "Too bad, it was your mistake and my good fortune." so he refused to bring it back. The cashier had to pay it out of her own pocket and lost her job on top of it. What a shame. It was the same kind of mistake, but a big difference. The two extremes still taught a lesson of honesty. Both stories have made a big impression on me.

I'm sure we all have had instances in our lives that have taught us valuable lessons. I encourage you to search your memories for such a lesson.

CHAPTER NINETEEN

Family Fashion Sense

We had a professional model in the family once who was my sister-in-law, Kathy Huang Sandberg, but I want to talk about the men in my family who had very high aspirations to always look their best. We were very proud of Kathy and her endeavors as a model and she modeled in New York and Chicago and has even been in moderate local shows in Florida recently. She also is a prominent Real Estate seller, and still works daily very hard at that even at eighty-four. We're all so very proud of her and her accomplishments.

I think my dad, Leonard Sandberg, has always had a sense of fashion and always wanted to dress with impeccable taste. He wore three-piece suits with flare as a young man and even as he aged, he was rarely seen without a tie. I was fascinated as a child at seeing his wing-tip shoes. I thought they were neat. He even wore dress shirts around the house much of the time.

My brother, Ralph, was so persnickety about his clothes, that he asked our mother to take his Army dress pants up just ¼ of an inch to meet his perfect eye. Who, but him, would have noticed that little difference?

Then there was my son, Jeff, who wanted only perfect all cotton dress shirts because they not only looked nice and elegant, but were pleasingly soft. But oh! The ironing was a chore. A little polyester mixed in with that cotton would have eliminated some of those wrinkles! His pants had to be just right too and Jeff would never go to church if he didn't have dress clothes with him or a suit. He never would have worn even a nice pair of jeans to church. I told him it didn't matter as folks wore any and everything today – even shorts! I told him God just cared if he would be there. It's a good thing I taught him how to to do laundry and iron before he went off to college. He had to dress up on his job too and learned he didn't want any one to do his laundry except him from there on out. He did allow me to occasionally iron for him cause he knew I would do it RIGHT!

You might call these excessively concerned men with their appearance and their taste to even be a bit foppish.

Most young men today don't usually care that much about what they wear. There is a lot more casualness today. I always enjoy seeing the men of my family impeccably dressed. I always helped pick my husband, Gene's clothes out, so he would always look nice and he always got complimented.

It shows the men of my family have great pride in their appearance.

Chapter Nineteen
Fashion-Dad

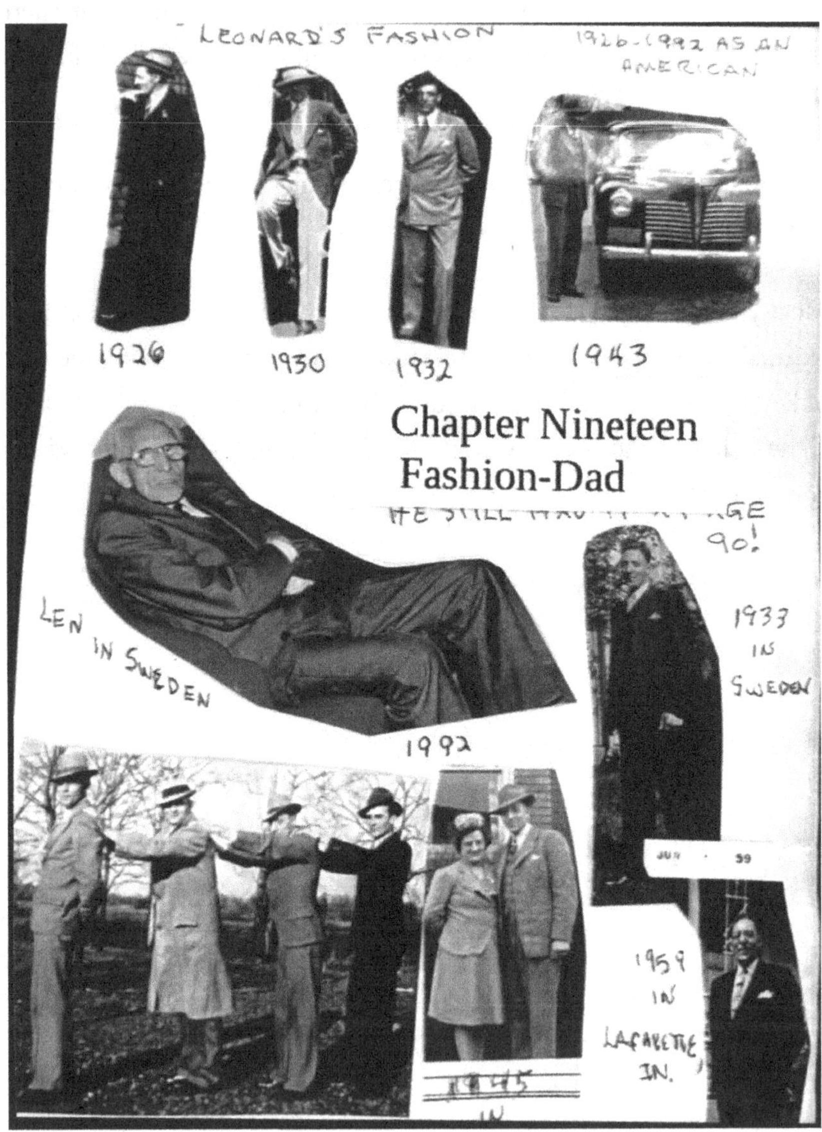

Chapter Nineteen
Fashion – Ralph

Chapter Nineteen- Jeff
All Spiffed up -2008

MARILYN IN FASHION

Chapter Nineteen
Fashion – Marilyn

Chapter Nineteen
Fashion – Kathy

Chapter Nineteen
Kathy is still a Model

CHAPTER TWENTY

My Dad's Work Influenced My Work

Jeremiah 29:11 "For I know the plans I have for you, declares the Lord, 'plans to prosper you and not to harm you, plans to give you hope and a future.'"

Hebrews 11:40 "God had planned something better for us so that only together with us would they be made perfect."

My Poem "WORK" January 10, 2023
By Marilyn Sandberg Grenat

"It was a joy to go to work every day,
And I was lucky enough to receive pay.

If we do it for the sake of serving our heavenly Father,
And do it without feeling it's a bother.

Serving mankind is not always easy,
But keep in mind we're serving Him above.
And we do this out of love.

My earthly father taught me good work ethics,
And I always gave my all in those endeavors.

Therefore I loved every varied job I had,
And never felt like any of them were bad.

What I didn't know, I strove to learn with zest,
So my results would always be my best."

Dad never felt like he couldn't accomplish something job-wise, so he always proceeded with the idea that he would succeed, and so he did. Even when his boss asked if he could weld. He had done some in his father's blacksmith shop, but he felt if he started to do more on the job he would learn more and do better and better, and so he did.

I took on this attitude when I started at the Sheiff's office, as I knew my office skills would carry me through, and I learned more about the law by reading, studying, and becoming friends with attorneys and the judges. I took some adult computer classes at Jefferson High School at night and went to paralegal school as well.

When I started my job at Purdue Accounting Department I had a lot to learn, but as usual, I was willing to do that. I was hired on as a supervisor, and I had to learn how to key data entry of many numbers, but I practiced until I got as good as the rest of the girls. Since I did it gradually, I learned to be extremely accurate, which won me kudos by my third boss. The first one was female and not neccessarily fond of me, because she always appeared to be jealous of others and would never take any of their suggestions to heart. My second boss was a young gal fresh out of college, and always very kind, but it was my third boss, an experienced male, who always seemed to give everyone a chance and gave me opportunities that showed my true abilities. He appreciated our efforts and was not shy about telling us so. It was a joy working for him and Purdue University.

While many old Swedes came from a farming background in Sweden, my paternal grandfather, Claes Magnus Sandberg, did not. He was the trusty, beloved blacksmith who kept all the horses shoed and the wagons and buggies in good shape and running smoothly. He even forged farming tools in his blacksmith shop. This is where all his three boys learned their tool making skills. It encouraged his eldest, Georg, to go on to create many inventions. He created a round stainless steel dishwasher in 1946, which was way before the time of our modern day knowledge of electric dishwashers. It wasn't until 1949 that automatic dishwashers were introduced into the home residences. He made metal dinner bells and I still have one today. He created metal statues, flower pot holders (which I have), water fountains and many more neat things. This is where my father learned his skills as a successful toolmaker that he brought with him to the United States.

His business school in Jonkoping enforced his abilities to become a savvy business man later in life. However, his on-going jobs experiences brought him to accomplish this feat of starting his successful business career. He established and started Sandberg Engineering Manufacturing Company as an engineering manufacturer's representative and kept it going for nearly thirty years from the 1950's to the 1980's. Mother, Helen, was his trusty well-accomplished secretary. Daddy always said he could never have done it alone. She took impeccable dictation and could type over 100 words a minute on a manual typewriter. She was a meticulous proof reader and her grammar was top notch. They were a perfect team in the business world.

Dad was always obtaining and contacting new vendors that could make anything or parts needed to make cars, airplanes, or any machine. One time he even had a job to make man-hole covers for the streets of Chicago. If a vendor wanted something made, Dad always knew another that could usually get the job done. It was not a job he was hired to do for any one person or company. It was a job he created himself and went out and approached companies to sell them on his services and then he would receive 5% to 10% on the jobs completed. He had to know these companies well, and he personally went to each one to see what their needs were and when he found vendors he had established in his list of capable vendors to do the job for them and would get them to make a quote on the price. It was very innovative and an intelligent idea. Who would have thought of such a thing. My dad was a great businessman and he knew how these things could be made and he knew the kinds of tools best to use and who had them.

He had worked many years in Lafayette, Indiana, Rockford, Illinois, Detroit, Michigan, Chicago, Illinois to name a few.

After marrying Helen Swanson, an American-Swedish girl, in 1935, in Lafayette. Indiana, they moved to Peoria, Illinois, where he went to work for Caterpillar Co. until 1946, after which he took his family to Sweden to live for a year. I worked many different jobs in my lifetime and I always put forth my best effort just like my dad did.

When I heard his story about saying he could do something he was actually willing to do better on the job, I did the same thing on my last job as I knew I could learn too on the next job. After all, I actually had to do a lot of learning on the previous job I had had and I learned it well, so I knew whatever I needed to learn on a new job, I would be capable of doing, thanks to my daddy and his encouragement.

His perseverance and persistence taught me to have the same when I took on any new job. It also helped in my last endeavor of starting my own business as a Caregiver for the young and the elderly. As one of our ministers mentioned it was a perfect job for me, as I truly enjoy helping others. Thus my ability to be “Daddy’s Girl”.

I enjoy telling a funny story daddy once shared with me in one of his trips in the 1970’s to a vendor to try to get their business. He traveled a lot especially in the beginning while he was developing his company as a manufacturer’s representative.

He said while he was talking to a perspective vendor, he leaned back in his straight chair and ended up on his back as the chair slipped out from under him. As it turned out both men had a good laugh and he ended up receiving him as a productive buyer. He kind of believed it was the chair accident that sealed the deal. Who knows. He was actually a very convincing businessman.

My poem "EIGHTY SHORT YEARS"
August 2, 2020 (3:30-4:30AM)

By Marilyn Sandberg Grenat

"I am short and sturdy and no longer thirty!
I am now eighty and not ready to call it quits
Even though I often give my kids the fits!

I've lived lots of years,
Through many joys and tears.

But I have a few more to go,
Even though I am getting slow.

I've seen many births and sadly a few deaths,
I've seen wars and celebrations,
Many birthdays, thanksgivings and Christmases.
I've lived many places,
Driven lots of different cars in all kinds of races.

The race of time,
Can be one of a kind.

I've driven in Indiana clear across country to California and New York....
've driven from North to South
Clear to the Gulf's mouth.

While I never saw the country numbers
That my son did, I still have seen quite a few even if in my slumbers.

I've experienced different cultures
Through the journey of books without the worry of vultures.

I've loved and I've lost
But not necessarily without cost.

I've lost to divorce and also death
And it maybe recorded by Macbeth.

I've enjoyed youth, daughtership, siblingship, wifeship, & motherhood.
My land, I've even been blessed with Grandma and Great Grandmahood.
Now that's a lot of blessings to behold-
And the stories that could be told.

I've loved my life as it's been full
But I still have more to do and fullfill.

I've completed two of my four books
That I've wanted to write and it looks

Like I am after all going to push forward
And try to do that as long as I don't slip backward.

Who would have ever known I'd eighty years reach,
But I want so much more to teach.

Hang in there with me kids of mine,
For I know I keep threatening to reach one hundred,
You hear of it happening more and more to each, and may I do that without having blundered.

Thank you for your safety and guidance my dear Lord,
May you give me continued health, peace, and this rich reward.

So I can give you all a story,
Before God takes me home to Glory."

By Marilyn Sandberg Grenat

Chapter Twenty
Dad the Business Man

CHAPTER TWENTY-ONE

My Business As A Caregiver For The Young &The Elderly

Colossians 3:23-24 "Whatever you do, work at it with all your heart, as working for the Lord, not for men, 24 since you know that you will receive an inheritance from the Lord as a reward. It is the Lord Christ you are serving."

My Poem "The Caregiver and the Client" April 26, 2018

By Marilyn Sandberg Grenat

"My clients are so special to me;
They make me as happy as can be,

Each day they wait and depend on my assistance,
While all the while there is no resistance.

I do for them as they request,
Always trying to do my best.

They need for me to fetch and carry,
And I never want to tarry.

They need groceries, necessities, and booties;
And I love to appease their desired duties.

They have appointments to meet,
And I love to march to their beat.

Doctors, friends, and hairdressers they want to see,
And to please, I will always take thee.

They may have cleaning or cooking needs,
So I always try to keep them up to speed.

Laundry is always a must,
And this I do with their trust.

We laugh, we talk,
And even sometimes walk.

The elderly or infirmed just need to be
Acknowledged and loved-don't you see.

Take time to provide
So all can abide
In perfect harmony."

Since I started a daycare for about four kids in my home in 2005 and continued to about 2010 for at least one who was my granddaughter, Corrine, until she went to daycare and then kindergarten, I suppose you could consider that my start of caregiving.

Actually, I took care of Gene from 1999-2010 as he had his Alzheimer's disease for eleven years.

After he passed in 2010, I started working for a caregiving company called "Homecare by Design" as a caregiver for about one and a half years. I watched an infant, several school-aged children and some elderly persons as well. After a year or more, I decided to give my notice to leave and start my own business.

It was the best decision and best job I ever had.

After ten years, I am still friends with the family of the infant that I watched before. The most wonderful part of working for yourself means you can consistently care for the same people and pick your places and people you serve. It's better for both sides when you can establish a constant clientele. New ones come and go as well and you establish many new friends.

I've taken care of Alzheimer patients, cancer patients, and one of my favorite clients was an ALS patient that I took care of for six years. The Covid epidemic came and the family felt they didn't want to risk folks coming to their home and possibly bringing the virus to sweet Carol. Her husband felt he could handle things on his own with the occasional help of two of his daughters. I've remained friends with their family to this day. All of these friendships will be very special to me forever. Most recently I took care of two newborns until they were a year old and could go to daycare. It was extremely special to me as they were my great granddaughters. They were a month apart. One was born in July and the other was born in August. They were cousins born to two sisters-my granddaughters. They were considered covid-time babies. We all stayed home a lot during that year.

Kelsey, my granddaughter, was mommy to Charlotte, born in July and Emily, Kelsey's sister, was mommy to Sylvia, born in August. These two little cousins were as different as could be. Sylvia had curly blond hair with big blue eyes and looked every bit the little Swede. Charlotte was born with a dark full head of straighter hair and big black eyes. They will probably grow up to drive the boys wild with their good looks. When their mommies asked me, their great grandmother (Momo), to come watch them for three days a week, I was estatic. What fun! It turned out to be just that. At first it was just Charlotte at her house and then Sylvia and her family came to stay too, so when it was both of them, it was like watching twins – very busy!

The cousins had so much fun together and played and jabbered with each other so sweetly. Now they are adjusting to their new separate day cares.

We had so much fun at Christmastime watching the three little cousins interact together. Owen, my grandson had a little boy, River, in June, so there are three darling one-year-olds.

I have finished caregiving for a period of time, so I can collect my thoughts and try to finish my third book – my autobiography - "Daddy's Girl".

Call MARILYN GRENAT

@ 1-765-742-7489

I can help with hygiene & dressing, light housekeeping, meal preparations, shopping needs, med reminders, laundry, & companionship.

Chapter Twenty-one Marilyn's Caregiver Services

GRENAT CAREGIVER SERVICES

Call MARILYN GRENAT

@1-765-742-7489

I can give a helping hand with heart to your shut-in in their home or independant living. I can help them stay at home where they are more

CHAPTER TWENTY-TWO

Different Perspectives – Through Others' Eyes

Ephesians l:5-7
Paul said God sees us as we are and beyond. He sees what we can be.

Ephesians 2:10 (NIV) "For we are God's workmanship, created in Christ Jesus to do good works, which God prepared in advance for us to do."

We meet many people through the years and we all view and see each other in a different manner. We can like or dislike some things about a person, but still enjoy their company. A friend suggested this chapter for my book which may give a different perspective of me. I liked that suggestion, as I know others may definitely see me in a different light than I see and know myself. It may be or may not be so flattering, and that's OK. I didn't ask folks for flattery, as you can see in my Foreword by my brother. He is a typical brother. I don't feel our parents ever showed any great favoritism to either one of us, but I did feel he got by with much more than I did. I always felt it was due to his charm and possibly his gender. It sounded like he thought I got better treatment. Fairly enough, the folks treated us both very kindly.

I suggested folks who have known me a while could write a few paragraphs depicting a remembrance they might have of me, so this first person is a first cousin of mine, so we have known each other for over fifty years.

1)."Marilyn is my favorite cousin. Her mother, Helen, and my father, Kenneth, were siblings. Because of distance between our families we did not visit too often. She is a very compassionate and caring human. On our visits to Lafayette, we visited Columbian Park. Such a great swimming pool and picnic area. Aunt Helen, Marilyn's mother, was a fabulous cook and baker. Marilyn and I still joke about before bedtime we relaxed with a soothing backrub, and I was always first to receive one. When it became her turn to receive one, I was asleep.

At the time of my Father's funeral, she hosted the out of town family. I remember her up all night preparing for the following day. Such an industrious person. This is my cousin Marilyn. I love her!"

Carol Swanson

2).For a period of time, I sold Mary Kay cosmetics, and Luana Meyers was my former Mary Kay distributor while she lived in Lafayette. She has since moved to Florida, but we have remained good friends and try to get together whenever she and Gary come to town.

"I would describe Marilyn as a person who always treats people with love and respect, looks on the bright side of every subject. She is someone who is a joy to be around. She wakes with a song in her heart and more spring in her step than the energizing bunny!

Marilyn is a gifted talented and lovely woman, who loves God, Family and friends with a passion! I've seen her face difficult times like a broken leg to a husband who didn't remember her name-or a son who passes way too soon. She knows God is on her side. It's a blessing to call her my friend.

I forget why the subject came up, but Marilyn said, "I wake up happy, Gene, her third husband, would make her laugh every day before she got out of bed and that impressed me as a great way to live life! ….And she has a beautiful laugh!

Thank you for asking me to share. Best wishes on the new books!"

Luana Meyers

3). This next family was a family I worked for about ten years ago and I was a Nanny to their 10 month-old baby for perhaps about two years. However, we have remained friends for about ten years now. They have a sweet little family of three boys now and live in a town south of here. The baby had separation anxiety at first, but we eventually grew very close as well. He was a sharp little guy and picked up his numbers and letters very quickly as I tried to help get him ready for day care and kindergarten.

They said, "Marilyn is the most well-rounded, cultured, loving, sweet, thoughtful, loyal, energized, hard-working, knowledgeable, well-spoken person they have ever met." They also said, "She was a great teacher and has a kind heart."

I have enjoyed watching their little family of boys growing up as we have remained friends. I have said I hope I live long enough to see the oldest graduate High School.

I want to thank the Royer family for your very kind words. I definitely appreciate your glowing rendition. I very much have enjoyed my association with your lovely little family.

Jacqueline & Ryan Royer

4). I worked at Purdue University in the Accounting Department for sixteen and a half years, and got to know a lovely gal in Property Accounting who also was my neighbor. We have remained friends since we quit work at Purdue and have both moved from the neighborhood.

We both had our eightieth birthdays in the past eight months, so we celebrated by going to dinner in April, 2021 at TC's - a favorite restaurant of ours in Battle Ground, In. where we had delicious prime rib.

It's been a pleasure to know and have Phyllis as my friend or over forty years.

She said, "I have known Marilyn for a number of years. She has always been very friendly and willing to help anyone. She was so supportive of her husband for years when he suffered decline in awareness. She was always very attentive, but also very warm and caring.

My memories are fading, but I remember one time when I stopped by and she was downsizing and moving into a smaller home. I helped for a while and she then insisted that she would cook lunch and I had to stay and eat. We both worked at Purdue and she was always ready to help anyone or share a smile or laugh."

Phyllis Smith

5). 4-26-2021

When I was in High School, there was a lovely family by the name of Osborn that lived across the street from us. They went to the same church, and the mother, Elma, was a friend of my mother.

I babysat for their girls for a while. Donna Osborn and I remained friends through the years even up to the year she retired from being a high school math teacher. Here is what she wrote:

"What I Love About You"

"Marilyn has been an inspiration to me for my whole life. When I was young, Marilyn was my really cool babysitter. She was so much fun, and beautiful. I wanted to be like her when I was a teenager.

When I was high school age, Marilyn was newly married, having children, and an integral part of Evangelical Covenant Church. Again, I admired her, this time for her strength as a young Christian woman and a loving mother.

As I grew into adulthood, I observed Marilyn and her relationship with her parents as they aged, her children and their families, and her son and his death; her loving and caring attitude showed me the way we should all treat our loved ones.

Finally, as my mother and I were living through her final years, I witnessed the truly loving kindness that she showed my mother. Marilyn visited my mom and shared memories from the old church, some of my mother's favorite years. As you can see, Marilyn has been an inspiration to me – her caring attitude toward everyone, her dedicated life with God, and her loving kindness for the elderly. I still want to be like her when I grow up."

Donna Osborn, retired HS teacher, Donna Osborn

....

6). This next person is a lady I met while working my Caregiver Services for a lovely lady who had ALS. She would replace me in the evening after I had been with the patient all afternoon for four days a week. We became very good friends through this endeavor.

"My friend Marilyn is first and foremost a great Christian. Her empathy and understanding of others with the ability to tell you truth is inspirational. I'm blessed to have her as one of my true friends who has never let me down. She reminds me of a hummingbird. She seems to have boundless energy and with a resting heart rate of 90-100 bpm; I think she's the human equivalent. I love her sense of humor and sage advice. I thank God for the day she came into my life. We met taking care of Carol with ALS and even though I moved two states away, we have remained friends. Marilyn, I love you dearly. When I grow up, I want to be just like you. God bless and keep you always."

Pam Russell

....

7). This next lovely person is a daughter of my former ALS patient/ client. Poor Carol had this awful disease for fourteen years, and I was with her for six of her last eight years. The only reason I didn't take care of her the last two years was because of the Covid-19 pandemic and her husband Jim felt he could handle her alone without any possibilities of someone possibly bringing in the new virus. His daughters continued to help him too, so he didn't have to do it all alone. Cheryl Steiner was one of their daughters and she sent me her paragraphs on a special day- Thanksgiving! It was most appropriate as she was thanking me and I, in turn, thanked her for the opportunity and privilege to care for both of her folks.

"A Special Lady in My Life" Thanksgiving 11-25-21

"Fourteen years ago my mother was diagnosed with ALS. After eight years of caregiving for her, my siblings and I just couldn't keep up with our lives and caregiving for mom. Marilyn entered into our lives when we decided to find someone to help. Although Marilyn was a bit older than both of my my parents, she brought a wonderful energy and sense of structure to my family that we desperately needed. She is the most loving, caring, trusting, and organized lady that I have ever met. She is my angel. I am forever grateful and Marilyn will always be a part of my family."

Love, Cheryl Steiner, daughter of Jim and Carol Waber (who was my client.)

....

8). This next person is my first blood granddaughter that has shown me great love and devotion through the years. She now, in fact, has shown me trustfulness by allowing me to be the nanny of my great granddaughter, Charlotte-her second child.

"One of the best memories I have with my Grandma (Momo) is when I went skydiving with her on her 75th birthday. Months before she had said it was on her bucket list and had always wanted to go, but no one would go with her. I immediately said I wanted to go with her, so we booked the trip with Indy Flights out of Frankfort, Indiana. It was considered one of the safest places to skydive in the Midwest. We had to be there early in the morning to go through the safety orientation, harness up and meet our instructors. We jumped tandem with two experienced paratroopers from Russia and Italy, I believe they were. I think we were a little nervous taking our flight up, and I kept looking over at Momo and wondering "WHAT THE HELL DID I GET MYSELF INTO," but sweet little Momo just kept smiling and having a great time. The time came when we were supposed to jump from the plane. Momo sat on the ledge of the plane, in her red pants and just like that, she was gone. So many thoughts ran through my head just thinking of all the things that could happen; I was terrified, but I don't back out when I say I'm going to do something. So, it was my turn to sit down on the ledge of the plane, the instructor counted to five, I closed my eyes and out the plane I went. We floated around in the air after a very brief free fall and all I could think of is Momo on the ground, what happened, am I dead, I can't breathe, this is awesome, just so many things. We landed safely and had the best time of our lives! Fun fact: Momo was concerned that we might pee our pants, so she bought us some Depends that we proudly wore as we jumped out of the plane!"

Kelsey Oswalt (Cohen), Granddaughter

This truly was an experience and fun thing to do with my trustworthy granddaughter. I will always treasure this experience for the rest of my life and each year since I have never been able to top this fun excursion. The next year I went horseback riding, then the next I bought a bike and I hadn't done either of them for thirty years, so I thought that was kind of brave of me. One more thing I want to do before I die, is go for a real balloon in a basket ride. I have been up in one with Gene and Corrine at Prairie Connor, but it was tethered, so we didn't go far-only up and down again.

9) This next granddaughter is Kelsey's sister and is the middle daughter of my middle daughter, Kristina.

She wrote this as a remembrance of some of our times together. "She said when she was a little girl, she and her sister, Kelsey, would stay at my house during the week while their dad worked and their mom went to school. She said she remembered how I made them salads for their late night snacks and oatmeal for breakfast. She said I would tell them bedtime stories of when I was a little girl and I also taught them some Swedish. I even told them the story of the 'Three Bears' in Swedish."

Emily Oswalt (Zanker), Granddaughter

10). This next person is my middle daughter.

"As a child growing up, we had many traditions. My mother is 100 percent Swedish as most of you know. We would celebrate a holiday in the Swedish tradition called 'Santa Lucia Day' on December 13th. She would dress up in a white gown with lit candles on her head and bring breakfast to our beds. We even played 'Santa Lucia' a few times at church too. Throughout the years she has surprised us a few times even though we are all gone and married. Traditionally, the eldest daughter would bring breakfast to the whole family.

With her having three daughters, we all over the years, have taken our turn being Santa Lucia, as have the granddaughters as well. Another tradition we always look forward to is her Swedish cooking. My sister, Jennifer, truly loves her Swedish pancakes (plattar), and cardamom coffee bread. My sister, Annette, still really likes her almond cookies (drommar). My brother, Jeffrey, loved her Swedish meatballs (kottbullar) and rice pudding. Honestly, I love them all. Maybe not her fruit soup (fruct soppa) is my favorite, but it was something she always made at Christmastime.

One other memory growing up in my family included late nights with my mom. When midnight struck, I would leave my bed to meet her in the kitchen, just the two of us. We would talk about my day while she made me a cinnamon toast snack. I remember her always singing. We'd rock in the rocking chair that was Grandma Brady's and she would sing me to sleep. These are all wonderful memories that I will cherish forever. Although there are many more, these memories are my favorite. My mother is truly a remarkable woman. I wouldn't be the person that I am without her in my life. God bless mothers that make an impact in their children's lives.

Thank you Lord for MY MOTHER!!! Mom, I'm so proud of you."

Love, Your Stina

(I use to call her that when she was little). And I treasure these same wonderful memories as well.

Kristina Fleeger (Oswalt)

11). This person is my third daughter and fourth child.

Mom Memories

"I couldn't have asked for a better mother to raise me. There are so many memories that I have and cherish, but one of my favorites would have to be when I was ten. My Swedish grandparents took me to Sweden with them for three long months. Being away from your mom that long at that age is......hard.

When we were set to fly home at the end of the summer, my mom was going to meet us at the O'Hare Chicago airport to pick us up. I was so excited to get off that plane, but instead, my uncle Ralph was standing there waiting for us. He tells me we're staying in Chicago overnight and driving home to Lafayette in the morning. That in itself, was as long as the three months I had been gone.

When we pulled into town I wanted them to go faster and run the red lights. As soon as we pulled into the driveway I don't think the car had even fully stopped and I was out of the car running to the front door. I remember my mom sitting on the couch reading the newspaper. I screamed "**MOM" and ran into her** arms. I don't think I let go for a long while. My best memory of it all was how she hugged me and how she smelled."

Thank you, Jenni (Fleeger)Delong

12.) This last person on my list is another daughter of Carol Waber, my ALS patient/client. - Cathy Jenkins July 22, 2022

I met Marilyn when my mom was sick with ALS. Marilyn helped care for my Mom (Carol) at our house. She was very sweet, caring, and helpful towards my mom. She helped me clean mom and dad's house, cooked meals, and brought happiness to our house. She was my angel when I was weak. I always enjoyed talking with Marilyn. She always encouraged me to do things and reminded me of how special I am. Marilyn's faith in God always made me continue to have faith when I was struggling. She has always been great to my three girls too. I enjoy my conversations with her. We don't see each other much since mom passed away.

However, she is always and will always be part of our family. She has a special place in my heart. We love her very much!

Take care, Cathy Waber Jenkins

CHAPTER TWENTY-THREE

Finality

If you've ever talked about your "lifeline" on your left hand down the middle of your palm, you can see that it's either smooth all the way or some irregular rough spots along the way. Mine does show some rough spots at the beginning and also at the ending, with a pretty smooth area through the middle. This pretty much has been my life so far. While it's true my beginning of life was a bit rocky for mother and me, I had a pretty smooth wonderful life through the first eighty years.

When I reached eighty, I found out why my back was giving me so much pain, while I do have arthritis of the spine and pretty much all through my body, I also have pinched nerves between my third and fourth vertebrae that causes my lower back pain and for my right leg to go numb from my ankle to my right knee and then my right leg gives out on me while I can't walk far or stand for more than a few minutes without my cane.

While Tina and I were in Sweden in 2022, I had to hang on to someone for support and now in 2023, I'm relying on my cane for short periods for support. My circulation in my feet in my feet and hands is also rather poor.

On top of that problem, I was diagnosed with breast cancer in my right breast and chose what I feel was the best breast cancer surgeon near Indianapolis, Indiana in the mid-west to operate on me in August, 2023, and he gave me a partial mastectomy. I then received twenty sessions of radiation with no need for chemotherapy from a fabulous team of radiologists in Lafayette, Indiana. The doctor said if I had to have cancer,

I got the best kind to get rid of and we caught it early, which was good. It was called "Ductal Carcinoma" (in situ- in place) stage zero. I still don't know if the radiation cured it or not completely, but I feel very positive about it with very little pain in that area. Now we're just waiting on a positive report from my oncologist.

The neurosurgeon decided not to do surgery on my back to fuse the bones together, as he said my bones are too soft with my Osteopenia, and that the screws would probably pull out and not hold any fusion.

It was decided by my pain specialist that I should probably not have a steroidal Cortisone shot just now as I had been taking Ibuprofen tablets for awhile. He had told me not to take any pain pills containing aspirin, which my Vanquish had. I laid off of those for a week as instructed, but since the Ibuprofen didn't have aspirin in it. I thought that would be okay. When I got to the surgery area for my shot, he said I could not get my shot because what I had been taking was a blood thinner and he said I could bleed out into my spine which could possibly cause permanent paralysis. Oh my! I felt bad that there was a team of four there waiting for me and I couldn't get my shot, so I have to wait two to three more weeks before I can get back in to get it. So I guess I go through Christmas in pain. They said I can only have Tylenol and they do absolutely nothing for me to relieve pain. I even read though that the stronger Tylenol could have some aspirin in it, so I will have to just try the weaker Tylenol to at least try to take the "edge" off. I have to lay off the pain meds for a whole week before the Cortisone shot, so guess I won't be doing much or going much for that week before. I'm scheduled for the first week in January now. I was not given written instructions ahead of time for what I could and couldn't do. I only was instructed not to take aspirin products.

I've heard from some that the shot doesn't always help for more than a month or so, or sometimes even at all. While I was hesitant at all to get the shot, I thought I should at least try it once to see if it would help. I think they will only give the shot every three months too. Here's hoping it gives me some relief. God is good and I'm relying on continued Blessing that He has given me all my life. I could see ahead of time by my "life line" that I may have a rocky end to my life, so it's a complete surprise. I still feel VERY BLESSED to have been given my so far eighty-three years of a Wonderful Life. I'm truly ready for my next life with my Heavenly Father!

I am now "CANCER FREE" HALLELUJAH!

Printed in the United States
by Baker & Taylor Publisher Services